HOW TO SAVE
MONEY

Richard Benson

SUMMERSDALE

Summersdale Publishers
46 West Street
Chichester
PO19 1RP
England

A CIP catalogue record for this book is available from the British Library.

Printed and bound in Great Britain by
Selwood Printing Ltd.

ISBN 1 873475 19 5

Illustrations by Sophie Sitwell

Contents

Introduction

This book is designed to help you in many ways. While its main objective is to save you money, precisely how much you wish to save depends on you. There are ways to save a little and other ways to make greater savings. Some require very little in the way of effort, others are not possible without a certain degree of sacrifice or compromise in your life.

Most of us do not earn as much as we think we need, and are constantly left wishing for that little bit extra. This book will not necessarily make you money, which is a different area altogether, but it will help you to utilise what money you do have more efficiently. The book contains valuable advice such as how to make more efficient use of your central heating system, and useful tips such as the secrets of getting a bargain, plus general hints on other areas of life that can save you money.

You may be familiar with many of the ideas mentioned in this book, but do you practice them? Saving money is a little like a régime or diet, it has to be followed strictly for any effect to be noticed. It will take a little while of following this book's advice before you reap the rewards, but it will be worth it in the end when you find you have more money (or fewer debts) than usual.

Not only will this book save you money, it should save time. As the old expression goes, 'time is money'. For some people this is quite literally true. Self employed people who charge for their services on an hourly basis can only earn as much as there are working hours in a week. If parts of their life take up too much time, it can mean less time available for work and hence less money. Saving time on household chores etc. can mean more money in the pocket at the end of the day.

One important aspect of this book is that many of the ideas and tips will not just be benefiting you, your actions could be helping to protect the environment, and conserving natural resources, particularly if you recycle waste products.

You might not be aware that every time we use electricity or gas in the home or drive a car we are probably having a detrimental effect on the planet. When fossil fuels are burnt they produce a by-product, carbon dioxide (CO_2). This is released into the atmosphere and is one of the causes of global warming, an increasingly serious and threatening phenomenon. Efforts are being made to reduce the emissions of harmful gases: many governments in the world have introduced strict policies to help reduce levels but individuals too can make a contribution. Roughly one quarter of the CO_2 produced in this country comes from domestic usage. Much electricity is produced by power stations from the burning of fossil fuels, so every time a light or a television is switched on the need for fuel is increased. Cutting energy usage in the home will make an important contribution to reducing global warming and other negative aspects of high energy use, and don't forget that if you are saving energy you will be also saving money!

However much media attention is given to the plight of the environment, are we really doing enough? If we compare our efforts with those of other countries such as Norway, Sweden or Germany, we appear shamefaced. There are hundreds of ways to make a contribution to this planet, but it seems that other countries are making faster progress towards a more energy conscious society than we are. One last message in this lecture: this is your planet, if everyone took the attitude,

'But it's not my problem', then we would be heading for disaster. Please give it some thought.

This book is not intended to turn us into Scrooges or to encourage us to live miserable existences. Hopefully it will have the opposite effect, making a positive contribution to your life, increasing your spending power, employing your resources more effectively so that the necessities of life are paid for with less money, leaving more funds free for the luxuries. Think about it: if you save a few pounds a week you could end up with enough saved at the end of the year to treat yourself to an extra holiday.

How To Manage Your Money

We have less and less real contact with our money these days. Salaries are normally paid directly into bank accounts because although there is nothing nicer than being handed a pile of cash it is more sensible and secure to have it paid in this way. This removes the temptation not to pay all of the money into the bank but to 'blow it all' straight away, and makes it easier to keep track of your finances.

The banks now offer services such as:

- Direct debit
- Standing orders
- Budget accounts.

These enable many expenses such as gas or electricity bills to be paid directly from your account by the bank. Subscriptions to journals or clubs can also be debited directly, without the need for you to write regular cheques. The advantages of these types of services are that they save you time, and take out the worry of remembering to pay certain bills. This in itself will save you money if you would otherwise be financially penalised for an overdue bill that had slipped your mind.

Paying with cash is becoming a thing of the past: even cheques are now being superseded by debit and credit cards in all but the smallest transactions. The general effect of 'paying with plastic' is to increase demand. Plastic does not feel like money, and the time delay between paying by credit card and actually receiving the bill means that many people spend more than they can really afford simply because it is so easy to do so. When the bill arrives, they are only asked to pay a minimum of, usually, 5% of the balance. This does not feel 'painful', and encourages full use of available credit.

Unfortunately, credit cards are an expensive way of borrowing. A prearranged overdraft at a bank is a cheaper way of borrowing than a balance on a credit card, and if your card balance becomes uncomfortably high you could save money in interest payments by paying off the card balance either with money from an overdraft or from a loan. If credit cards are used with restraint, however, they can save you money. If your bank account is not in credit and you wish to purchase something, buying it with a credit card gives you at least a month's interest free credit. If you then pay the balance in full at the end of this interest free period, it means you have avoided paying a little extra interest on your overdraft during this period.

Never borrow more than you can comfortably repay

Budgeting

In an ideal world it would be nice not to have to worry about money. However, it appears that regardless of how much we earn we spend right up to our limit and often over it. No matter how many possessions we own or how many holidays we take we always seem to want more. If you are not like this then you are lucky! We may not all be greedy, but it is human nature to want more. So the solution is to be more careful with our money.

If you have an idea of exactly how you spend your income it will be easier to make adjustments to your expenditure. But as we seem to have little actual contact with our money it is often harder to control. That is the advantage of using cash as a primary method of payment: you can actually feel and see the money leaving you. This is always painful and you might be less inclined to fritter it away than if you were paying with a credit card. The best advice if you cannot control your spending is to take a pair of scissors and cut up your cards and stick to paying with cash.

Your current situation

It is a good idea to begin your efforts towards saving money with a financial overhaul. The first stage is to work out what money you have coming in, if you have a partner do a joint calculation. Possible sources of income are, for example:

- Wages
- Pension
- Investment Income
- Income Support
- Sickness Benefit
- Invalidity Benefit
- Housing Benefit

The next stage is to try and work out what your expenses are for an average month. If you write down all your various expenses it is then easier to begin to think about cutting down in certain areas. If you have no record of what you have been spending it is much harder to do this. The best thing is to keep a written record of all expenses, covering everything during the next thirty days. Provided nothing too exceptional was bought during this period, it will be alright to use this as an average month.

Keep a record of all expenses

Many people are quite content to avoid all possible thought of how they spend their money because they feel guilty at what they have been spending their money on, or because they don't realise that by paying attention to where it goes they could save a fortune. If you write down and look carefully at your expenditure then you will be more inclined to make some sort of effort to make a few cutbacks. It is not always possible to account for every penny but here is a list of some of the most commonly incurred expenses:

● **Food**
As well as the regular weekly shopping make a note of how much is spent on occasional snacks, drinks, sweets and meals out. This can often be equal to or in excess of the amount spent in the supermarket, and represents an area with huge potential for economising.

● **Motoring**

● **Travel expenses**

● **Household necessities**
Mortgage or rent, council tax, phone bill, television licence, energy bills.

● **Other necessities**
Credit repayments, insurance, assurance etc.

● **Entertainment**

● **Holidays**

● **Newspapers**

- **Saving**

- **Sundries**

Also include a list of debts, such as money owed on:

  - Credit cards
  - Hire Purchase
  - Overdrafts
  - Loans
  - Mortgages

Any money that is borrowed will be costing you money in interest. In some cases, extortionate rates of interest are charged.

The above list covers a range of expenses. Some of them are referred to as **fixed costs**, such as mortgage repayments, council tax, hire purchase instalments, insurances etc. These fixed costs are normally paid at fixed times, so you know when to budget for the expense. The other type of costs is **variable costs**, and as their name implies they change according to usage, like heating or electricity.

You should work out how much your fixed expenses are and set aside an appropriate amount of money for these, then you can work out how much you have to spend on the variable expenses, over which you have some control.

It is sensible to keep an accounts book, not just the back of an envelope, as being organised is one of the secrets of saving money.

Using past bills write down your expenses for the previous year, if available, in order to give you an idea of what to budget for this year. This is useful because some expenses are seasonally variable: gas bills, for example, are higher in winter than in summer, so knowing only what the average gas bill is may leave you short when the winter bill arrives as it will be way above average.

Past bills will give you an awareness of roughly what to budget for, taking into account inflation and other factors of course. No two years will ever be the same, but an approximate guide is better than no guide. The first step towards saving money when looking at the year as a whole is to have a reasonable idea of how much the main expenses will be. When budgeting for this year on the basis of last year, try to add a couple of percentage points above the rate of inflation in order to cover yourself against inevitable price rises.

Balancing the accounts

In theory the amount of money coming in should tally with the amount of money going out. However, this is living on the edge as there are always expenses which you cannot plan for and therefore savings are needed to cover these eventualities.

For those who find surviving on their income a constant battle, remember you are not alone. In fact, getting into debt is not at all uncommon. If you are still in control of your debt, i.e. you can cover the repayments, then this is not so bad. But for many the debts spiral and can eventually lead to serious problems such as homes being repossessed or having the bailiffs enter your house and remove your possessions in order to recover bad debts. This is a devastating experience that should be avoided at all costs. In order to avoid slipping into the 'debt trap' keep a watchful eye on your expenditure and never borrow more than you can afford comfortably to repay.

If you are struggling to make ends meet there are two simple choices:

• *Choice 1 is to increase your income.*

• *Choice 2 is to reduce your expenditure. Making the money you earn go further will have a similarly beneficial effect.*

It all sounds easy in theory, but in reality whichever choice you make will require willpower and effort to achieve. Just remember that although changing your expenditure habits in order to avoid debt may not be easy, it is far easier to go out of your way to walk around a hole than to try to climb out of it once you have fallen in. Debt can be like that, and is better avoided in the first place.

This book's aim is not really to tell you how to increase your income, but there are tips here and there throughout the book which may be of use. Primarily it is concerned with choice number 2, reducing expenditure, but in a way that will not be painful, complicated or difficult. Anyone can make easy savings if they know how.

Paying Bills

A brown envelope popping through the letter box is rarely good news. In fact the majority of post seems to be either bills or junk mail, and the bills can cause a real headache if not downright despair. But if you are organised you will find that it is easier to make the payments, and paying on time will avoid penalties and save money. Most of the utility companies do not take kindly to late or nonpayment and their punishment for this sort of behaviour is often to cut off the service they provide. This not only leaves you very inconvenienced but it will cost you even more money when you have to pay to be reconnected.

Some bills, such as those for electricity and gas, are often worked out as an estimate. This means that the company calculates a new bill using past bills as a guideline to what amount they expect you to have used.

The first thing to do when you have opened your bill is to check the estimated figure with the true reading. If the estimate is way off the mark, either too high or too low then the money they are requesting will be wrong. Obviously if their estimate is much higher than the actual reading you will be paying more than you have to, and I'm sure you would rather have the use of that money yourself. If the estimate is only marginally out, there is no point in having your bill altered, but if it is a significant amount of money then you can send the company in question a true reading and they should send you a revised bill. If the bill they sent you is too low then you are not obliged to inform them, it just means that when they do read the meter your next bill will be that much larger, so be prepared.

If the bill you receive is higher than you believe it should be, don't just accept it as being automatically correct as you could be paying more than you should. There was a case where a man received a phone bill for a period when he was away, he queried this with BT, and eventually they found that due to some faulty wiring his line and another person's had been mixed and for years they had been paying each other's bills.

> # Always check your bills thoroughly: mistakes can occur

There are thousands of queries every year for most of the utility companies, so it is certainly not a quick procedure getting something investigated. The company will often be adamant that there is no problem. Keep on persevering until they do listen, or contact the official body that governs their conduct if you have no luck.

One common problem stems from inaccurate meters. If you believe the bill is higher than it should be it is usually possible to have the meter checked. However, there is a drawback to this approach: before you think about having this done, bear in mind that if the company checks the meter and they find there are no faults with it then you will have to pay them. This varies from company to company, but is around £20 to £30.

Paying the utility companies

Most people are connected to the electricity, water and gas supplies. Life would be exceedingly difficult without them, but these luxuries have to be paid for. Most of the companies send out quarterly bills, which have to be settled within a certain period. Some companies allow payment to be made through a direct debit scheme, which is convenient and can be cheaper if the company offers discounts for direct debit.

There are also 'budget plan' schemes that are designed to spread the cost of your bills over the year, instead of having to pay them in large amounts. It sounds fine until you begin to think about it: instead of paying quarterly you will pay monthly instalments, and this means that you will be paying them in advance. It makes better financial sense to save the money yourself and put it in a savings account so that at least you get the interest on your own money before you pay the bill. The only advantage of these 'budget plans' is that they are helpful for people who find it hard to save or manage their finances.

Standing Order
This is an instruction that you give to your bank to pay a fixed amount from your account on agreed dates.

Direct Debit
This gives an organisation the right to withdraw money from your account at agreed times. This is useful for paying for things such as car insurance.

Cutting Costs

Electricity
It is possible to make use of cheap electricity. Economy 7 is electricity supplied during off peak hours, but you need to have a special meter fitted and there is a higher standard charge per quarter than normal tariff electricity, currently about £3 extra. How much cheaper the electricity is varies from company to company, but it is on average

about 5 pence a unit cheaper during the off peak hours. Beware - some companies charge more for the normal rate. Economy 7 is most beneficial for homes with storage heaters that consume a large amount of electricity during the night.

Water Meters
It is now standard policy for many of the water companies to fit water meters so that they can calculate how much water a household uses and then charge according to usage. As with any change of policy it has aroused public concern. Prior to the water meters the bill was a fixed amount regardless of usage. There was no need to worry about using a sprinkler on the lawn and you could have as many baths as you had hot water. Sadly for many these days are over.

For those who are cautious with their water supply, having a water meter might work out cheaper than the old system, but for many having to be economical with water usage is a burden. If you do not have a meter there is no compulsion to economise on water usage, however if you have a meter there will always be the thought that if you use less water the bill will be cheaper.

If you have a water meter and you want to cut your bill here are some tips:

● Take showers, not baths.

● Do not use a sprinkler on the garden.

- Use the washing machine only for full loads.

- Only use the dishwasher once a day.

- Mend dripping taps.

- Recycle water from the house and collect rain water in rain butts.

- Put a brick in the toilet cistern so that it uses less water to flush, or install a toilet with a dual flush system.

- Keep drinking water chilled in the fridge instead of running the tap until it is cold.

Shopping

The temptation to spend money whilst out shopping is hard to resist. The charms of clever advertising can lure all but the very strong into buying those products which at the time might have seemed like a good idea but when you arrive home you begin to wonder why on earth you parted with your money. There are many cardinal rules that must be obeyed before commencing a shopping trip, and these are outlined in this chapter.

Always make a list of what you intend to buy. This will save you time trying to remember exactly what you came out for. Also, if you don't make a list, it is easy to forget an essential item that will result in a second trip being made. Yet another waste of time and money.

Resist temptation

If you are a compulsive shopper i.e. you can't help buying things you don't really need, try to control these compulsions. Before you pick anything up think to yourself 'do I really need that?' If you are still tempted, go away and think about it. Quite often you might come back and think, 'well I didn't really have any use for that after all'.

Bargain prices

Who can resist a bargain? The shops seem to go from one sale to another. With discounts of 30-60% commonly advertised, it all sounds too good to be true. The allure of sale items is immense and the satisfaction of getting a 'bargain' is rewarding. There is, however, a number of rules to learn before you commence your bargain hunting.

● Set yourself a limit on how much you are going to spend and don't go over this limit.

● Check that the goods you wish to purchase are not damaged or faulty, or you are at least aware of the condition of the product. Many sale items are seconds or damaged stock so they might not be as much of a bargain as you might think.

● Check whether you can return the product if you are not satisfied with it, e.g. if you buy a new jacket but are not sure about the colour, ask them if they will give a refund if you return it.

● Shops are not obliged by law to exchange or refund goods simply because you later decide that you don't like the colour or the style, but many shops have the decency to go beyond their statutory duties in the name of customer care. Your statutory rights ensure that you have the right to a refund if a good purchased is not fit for its stated purpose, or had been described prior to the sale in a misleading way. A simple change of mind after a purchase does not give you the right to a refund, but many shops care sufficiently for customer relations to offer refunds voluntarily.

• Check the prices of the same product in other stores. If you find it at the same price in another store, tell them and they should try to beat that price.

• Try for a further reduction in the price, as they are often open to dropping the price even more if you make the effort to ask. This is not so much the case with the chain stores, but individual shops have more flexibility.

• Never appear too eager when enquiring about a product that you know you want. If they know that you are definitely going to buy the product they know that they will not have to drop the price for you. It is better to appear only mildly interested, then say 'Well, I might be interested if the price could be lowered'. They will either laugh at you or come to a compromise that you are more than happy with.

● Check that the product you are buying comes with a guarantee.

● Think carefully if you really need it. Do you have the room and time to make use of it, or is it going to be stuck in the garage in a few months? If you have ever bought a piece of exercise equipment, you will be familiar with such a scenario.

● Don't lose your judgement.

Bargains are not always what they seem.
Everybody likes to pick up a bargain: it makes you feel good. Many people end up spending the money they saved with a bargain on something additional. The second purchase is justified in their eyes because they made a saving on the first product. If you do this you will be no better off financially but you are not spending any more money than you would originally have done and you have managed to buy 'two for the price of one'.

> # Make sure your bargain is really a bargain by checking the prices elsewhere before purchasing

Bargains can have their downsides, unfortunately. Many people lose all sense of control in shops where goods are reduced, and the cuts in price can encourage people to buy items that they do not need and on reflection do not really want, but as there is a substantial saving on the item they feel they cannot pass up such an offer.

Shopping for Food

Food, glorious food - cream cakes, fresh strawberries, smoked salmon or bangers and mash: whatever your fancy you can't live without food. The weekly food bill for many people is one of the biggest outgoings that they incur. Bills of over £100 for a family of four are now not uncommon.

It is becoming easier and easier to spend large sums of money at the supermarket, and this is due to certain factors in addition to the fact that food prices have risen steadily. There are many expensive products that would once have been regarded as a luxury which are now commonplace in a shopper's basket.

People often now value time more than they do money, with the inevitable result that convenience foods such as prepackaged meals and ready prepared vegetables are bought in vast quantities regardless of the expense.

Not all shoppers realise that they are paying twice as much or more for this convenience than they would pay if they bought the 'raw materials' rather than the finished product. Do you really want to pay someone in a factory to prepare your meal rather than prepare it yourself at a fraction of the cost? If you are keen to save money on a regular basis prepare to change your shopping habits. Many people who get accustomed to convenience shopping may suddenly find it tough if they experience a drop in earnings for any reason.

Try not to spend too much on convenience foods

Shopping saver tips

Always make a thorough list of all the food products you need before you embark on your shopping trip. It will help you to save time as you won't have to think what you came out for. If you don't make a list you might forget an important item then you will have to make a return trip wasting further time and money.

Try to resist temptation. Buy what you really need and discard any items that you can live without.

However this does not mean that you have to forgo all gastronomic luxuries: try to regard them as treats as opposed to necessities.

Always buy vegetables and fruit that are loose rather than prepackaged. Although these prepackaged items come ready washed, how long does it really take to wash them? Is it worth paying the extra? On average they are about 20% more expensive. If you work out how much you might spend just on vegetables it is surprising how much you would save.

Look out for special offers in all departments. There are often a few lines in each supermarket that are actually sold at a loss, usually changing from week to week or month to month. If you buy the specials and adjust your menu accordingly, you will save a small fortune.

Some stores also offer reductions for buying a number of the same item eg. buy three get one free. Stock up on these items if they are things that you use regularly, but if it is an obscure or a luxury product it is probably not worth your while.

It is a good idea to take a calculator when shopping. You can then work out exactly how much you are spending. It is easy to get a shock at the till when the total bill comes up, but with a calculator you will know how much it will be. It also makes it easier to budget as without a calculator it is hard to know exactly how much you are spending.

Cut out money-off coupons from magazines and newspapers. If you look hard enough there are literally hundreds, not only for food but for a whole range of products.

If you are a real bargain hunter find out what time your local supermarket reduces the prices of its perishables. Many items such as meat, fish, fruit, vegetables and bread are marked down. If you have room in your freezer and you find some real bargains, buy them and stick them in the freezer to use at a later date.

Supermarkets often have a section where they sell damaged stock off cheaply, but it is not advisable to buy dented tins of meat or fish.

Try to avoid going shopping when you are hungry. Shopping on a full stomach means that you are less tempted by appetising looking food products that you would not normally buy. Buying a bar of chocolate to eat before going into a supermarket could actually save you money if it stops you buying excessive quantities of sweet items inside.

Instead of buying ready made meals such as chilli con carne or lasagna which are tempting if you are not in the mood for cooking, make your own on a day when you are not busy and freeze them for a later date. This is very much cheaper than buying ready made meals, especially if you make them in bulk. Also, by making your own you will know exactly what ingredients you have put in the food.

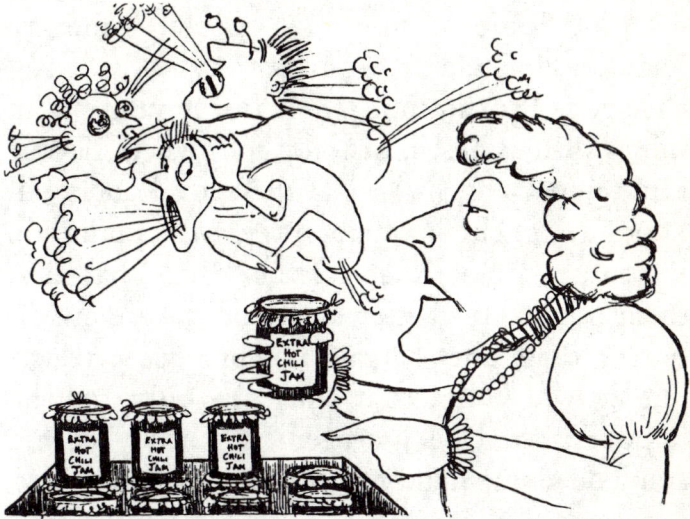

Stick to the supermarket's own brands of goods, unless an individual manufacturer has goods on a special offer that makes them cheaper than anything else. There can be a big difference between the prices of branded and non-branded foods: on average they are about 20% less. If you bought most of the essential items such as rice, cereals and bread as non-branded products you would save pounds off your weekly food bill. Own brand goods are usually just as palatable as the real thing: often they are manufactured by the same company in the first place, being identical products with different packaging. Try a few of the products and see if you notice any difference. If you really find one or two unappetising then go back to your old products for those, but buy the ones you do like.

Loss leaders

Some supermarket chains even sell extra low price own brand goods at a loss or at a very small profit margin. Some of them are edible, some are revolting, but the prices make you feel as if you have gone back in time ten or fifteen years. With things such as bleach or toilet rolls where flavour is not important, sticking to these loss leaders will knock a large chunk off your weekly shopping bill. If you can stomach any of the 'edible' bargains, then so much the better. Many people are put off buying these ultra bargain non-branded products due to the belief that they are only for the impoverished. Does it matter that much when you could be saving hundreds of pounds a year?

> # Don't be put off by plain packaging if the product is cheap

Discount Food Stores

A number of discount food stores are starting to appear in this country. Many are owned by foreign food chains that have seen a gap in the market. They can be described as cheap and cheerful, they dispense with the frills and just stock the essentials, but many of the items have to be bought in bulk. As for cost, they are not always as cheap as they appear to look. It is worth comparing their prices with your local supermarket as they are often pretty close in price and the supermarket may even be cheaper. The interiors of these discount food stores are bare and they exude a sense of frugality, but remember that appearances can be deceptive.

The latest import from America, where as we know everything occurs in a big way, is warehouse shopping. I still find it hard to understand why the Americans use large paper sacks with no handles to carry their shopping, and refer to shopping trolleys as karts, funny lot those Americans. Anyway, back to the warehouse shopping, at present there is only a couple of such places in this country, but if they prove to be as popular as the ones across the water then we can expect many more over the next few years.

If you have not heard of them, here is a quick resumé. They are big, huge, Gargantuan, they make your average Sainsbury's seem like a local corner shop. They offer a wide range of products, food, electrical goods and clothes, all at discount prices. If it all sounds too good to be true, well, there are drawbacks. They are not open to the general public as they are designed for small businesses, and people in certain professions. There is also an annual charge made for using the shopping facility. The last drawback is that you have to buy many of the items in bulk.

Markets

Most towns and cities still have traditional markets where it is possible to buy a variety of goods, ranging from fruit and vegetables, meat, clothes, and tools, all at economical prices. Some markets still have livestock sales which are fascinating spectacles to watch.

Most markets start bright and early in the morning and finish about 3pm. At the end of the day the prices of many items are reduced especially on the fruit and veg stalls, so it is the ideal time to pick up a few bargains.

Kitchen

There are savings to be made in the kitchen both in terms of time, money and the environment. Some of these points may seem obvious or you might already practice them but there is no harm in reiterating these simple savers.

● Don't overdo it on the washing up liquid. Most detergents are concentrated and only need a minute amount. Don't squeeze them into oblivion!

● When hand washing either dishes or clothes, always wash from the cleanest to the dirtiest items. This will save both water and detergent.

● Always use a washing up bowl, rather than using the sink. This requires less water to fill: in particular, less hot water, which is expensive. It also allows rinsing (in cold water) exceptionally dirty items over the side of the bowl if you only have a single sink unit, before putting them into the bowl. This keeps dirt out of the bowl and means you are less likely to have to change the hot water.

● Do not wash anything under a hot running tap when you have the plug out.

● Never boil more water than you require: it is waste of water and fuel. If you are making a drink for one it is more cost effective to boil the water in a saucepan (with the lid on, of course) on a gas cooker rather than to use an electric kettle.

● Use a vegetable steamer so it is possible to cook all your vegetables in one pan as opposed to using a number of pans.

● A pressure cooker is a very efficient method of cooking and a number of items can be prepared quickly and easily.

● If you have a gas cooker do not let the flames lick around the edge of a saucepan. This is a waste of fuel and it can ruin your pan. If you have an electric stove, choose an appropriate size ring if you have a choice.

● When using the oven, try to make full use of it. Vegetables can be cooked along with the main course to avoid using the rings. Once you get the hang of cooking many different things together, you will find it will save you time and reduce the amount you have to wash up. Dishes such as casseroles are ideal for cooking in an oven and it is hard to overcook a casserole! If the oven is being used for baking, why not prepare two or three times the original amount and freeze the extra if possible. It will save time in preparation and fuel.

● It is possible to turn the oven off 10-15 minutes before the dish has finished cooking as the oven will retain enough heat to finish the dish off. This only applies to dishes that require a long period of cooking, i.e. over 1 hour, and always double check that the dish is sufficiently cooked.

● Try to keep the lids on pans when you are cooking, unless it specifies in the recipe that you should keep the lid off.

● The smaller you cut your food up the quicker it will cook, saving you precious time and money.

● If you know in advance that you will be cooking something from the freezer, put the food in the fridge to let it defrost thoroughly before cooking. It will cook faster and use less energy.

Appliances

There appears to be a never ending array of new kitchen gadgets that are available on the market, many of them imports. As well as the more common blenders and food mixers, there are gadgets such as juicers, cappuccino machines, rice cookers, slow cookers . . . the list is endless.

Although the plus side of this that many of them save you time and are fun to use, there is the added problem of storing all these gadgets and many of them require electricity. Only buy or use appliances that you feel are essential and that you can afford to operate.

Dishwasher

So OK this is one gadget that we all want and would find it hard to do without once we have one, but there is the temptation to over-use it. Only use the dishwasher once a day, it is much more efficient to stack the dirty plates from the day's meals and switch the machine on in the evening. If you are trying really to tighten those purse strings, you could even consider doing the dishes manually. (What a suggestion!)

Tumble dryer

This is one invention that is incredibly useful in this wet country. Having to put the washing out truly is a chore, especially when it starts raining ten minutes later. So why not just stuff all that wet washing in the tumble dryer and forget the weather? Well, one reason for not using a tumble dryer is that it is expensive to run. If you do own one try to use it only when really necessary. If the weather is fine and you have a garden save yourself some money and put your clothes out on the line. There are some tumble dryers on the market that can sense when the clothes are dry and turn themselves off automatically. Remember do not overfill your tumble dryer as it will not dry the clothes as efficiently.

One other consideration that should be noted is that when clothes are dried in a tumble dryer they deposit a substantial amount of fluff. This is made up of the fibres from the clothes, indicating that during the drying process they do wear out more quickly than if they were dried on a washing line, due to the friction involved. *So not only is the tumble dryer an expensive choice in terms of energy consumption, it also means clothes will need replacing sooner.*

Fridges and freezers

● Always site your fridge and freezer in the coolest possible place in your kitchen. If your fridge or freezer is next to your cooker it will have to work much harder to keep the temperature down.

● Remember to place your appliance at least an inch from the wall to allow cool air to circulate and hot air to escape from the back.

● Never leave the doors open to the fridge or freezer longer than you have to, and avoid placing warm food in them as it will cause the temperature to rise and take more energy to lower it again.

● Once in a while check the seals for tears and give the seals a clean.

● Defrost your fridge and freezer regularly, as they do not run efficiently if they are iced up.

Running Costs of Kitchen Appliances

When purchasing a new kitchen appliance such as a fridge or freezer the main considerations are usually the price along with styling and size. But do you ever consider the running costs of the appliance? This is actually very significant due to the extensive differences in running costs between similar appliances, so although two similar appliances might vary in price by £20 and most people would choose the cheaper one, you could find that the more expensive appliance would be £20 a year cheaper to operate. Now think about how long the average kitchen appliance would last, say, ten years. It could then save you £200 over the other appliance which originally seemed the better buy. The long term saving could effectively repay the entire original purchase.

Manufacturers until recently have not been very forthcoming with information on energy usage, which makes it difficult when considering what appliance to purchase. All new appliances such as fridges and freezers now have to come with information giving details of their energy consumption, efficiency and noise. Magazines such as 'Which' often print reviews on household appliances giving information about which of them are the best buys and useful figures regarding how much they cost to run.

The difference between the most efficient and inefficient appliances can be between 50% and 100%, so you could save a small fortune over the lifetime of the appliance even if it does mean spending a little more at the time of purchase.

Don't always think just about the purchase price of an appliance, consider how much it will cost to run

Most houses are filled with numerous electrical appliances, and many of these are constantly on 'stand-by' such as televisions, video recorders, and kettles. These appliances are all drawing power and can account for over 10% of the average electricity bill. These items should be switched off when not in use, which would also reduce the risk of electrical fire.

Energy Savers

Central Heating

There are people who still claim that we were better off before the advent of central heating. This sort of statement is normally accompanied by comments such as 'No one got colds until they had central heating put in' or 'In my day we used to rub two sticks together to keep warm'. Whatever happened in history, central heating is now commonplace in most homes. Those who want to live without it and use an outside toilet are welcome to do so.

Having central heating does not mean that your home has to be the same as the interior of a sauna. The temperature can be controlled to a climate in which you feel comfortable. If you want to put on your swimming costume and pretend that you are in the Caribbean then turn up that thermostat, sit yourself down in your deck chair with your feet in a bowl of sand, and sip your favourite cocktail. While this is possible, such mid-winter armchair holidays can cost as much in heating bills as it would actually to go there. Central heating is expensive to run and is one of the most significant areas of potential savings.

Central heating systems use a variety of domestic fuels. The most popular choice is gas, followed by electricity, although oil is still used as are solid fuels such as coal or wood. (Nuclear reactors in the home are not recommended).

Hot tips on cooling your fuel bills

● Have your boiler serviced regularly. This will not only make it run more efficiently but it will also be safer. Safety should never be compromised in the pursuit of saving money.

● Try reducing the temperature by one degree at a time until you begin to feel chilly. It is estimated that if you reduce the temperature on your heating control by one degree all year you will save between five and ten per cent of your annual fuel bill. This is a significant saving for the sake of one degree.

● Remember to switch your heating off when you don't need it. If you know that you are going out for the day, then either turn it off or turn it down low so that it keeps the house from getting cold but you are not wasting too much money and precious fuel.

● If your heating system runs on oil or solid fuel make enquiries about buying a quantity during the summer months, as you should receive a reduction in price. Offer them cash and you might get an even bigger reduction.

● Set the timer clock for your central heating carefully. If you can make do with the heating coming on 10 minutes later and going off 10 minutes earlier than normal, the saving will add up to a worthwhile sum of money over a year.

● It is essential that your central heating system has a timer and thermostat at the very least. It would be preferable to fit individual thermostats on the radiators. One cause of inefficiency is due to the fact that most houses only have one thermostat and this controls the output for the whole house, and this causes a number of problems.

● There are huge savings to be made by having an energy efficient home, it will also help the environment.

● If the thermostat is situated in either a particularly warm or cool room, the house will be heated according to the temperature in that room. This could mean that your house is either under or over heated. By fitting thermostatic radiator valves

(TRVs) a more accurate and efficient control can be achieved. It is then possible to set the temperature for each individual room, because certain rooms need to be warmer than others: living rooms are normally kept at a higher temperature than hallways, for instance. If you can set the required temperature for each room it will not only save you money but you will feel more comfortable with the level of heat.

● So what do they cost? The TRVs cost from about £9 for a mechanical model, and a more sophisticated electronic version is available at around £50. The electronic version can be programmed to come on when required and the temperature is easier to adjust.

● The drawback to TRVs is that although they look fairly simple, they are rather difficult to fit and it would be necessary to have them fitted by a plumber, unless you are very competent at plumbing yourself. If TRVs are fitted to a standard sized three bedroom house a saving of around £15 a year would be made.

The central heating boiler is like the heart of the human body, the life source of a house that provides hot water and warmth. The pipes in a house are like the arteries in the body, but instead of carrying blood, the pipes are carrying hot water, oil or air. To continue with this analogy, the condition of the boiler is as vital for a house as is the human heart for our body. Many old boilers do not work efficiently, especially if they have not been regularly maintained, and this is a terrible waste of fuel.

● When your boiler is next due for a service ask the engineer to see how efficient it is. It is now possible to buy more energy efficient boilers than ever before: a condensing boiler is the most efficient and although it will cost more than a standard model it could save you over a £100 a year on your heating bill. This is quite a substantial saving and it will go on saving you money year after year. New boilers tend to be smaller giving you more room.

● Make use of cheap electricity if your central heating system is electric. Economy 7 is charged at around half the price of regular electricity. A special meter has to be installed, but is ideal for homes that use night storage heaters.

● If you use a radiant fire with a reflective metal shield make sure that you polish the shield. If it is dull it will not reflect the heat as efficiently.

● Buy heaters and other winter items such as heavy duty quilts in the summer when they may be cheaper.

Energy-Saving Lightbulbs

It is now possible to replace ordinary filament lightbulbs with compact fluorescent lightbulbs. They are ideal for use on lighting appliances that are used frequently and for long periods, such as in halls or living rooms. You might think that the cost of using an ordinary filament bulb is minimal, but when you begin to think how many lights the average house has and how long they are used for, the cost adds up.

An energy saving bulb uses roughly three quarters of the electricity of a conventional bulb and will last on average eight times as long. A lightbulb can be on for about 6 hours a day. Therefore, an energy-saving bulb effectively can have paid for itself within one year. There are other advantages such as if they are fitted in awkward places, it will cause less inconvenience because they have to be fitted less often. This is particularly good for the elderly: fitting lightbulbs causes numerous accidents each year, normally from people falling off chairs.

Energy-saving lightbulbs are widely available, with both the screw-type and bayonet fittings. They also come in a variety of shapes, sizes and ratings. Depending on the shape of the bulb the pattern of light is affected. The 'stick' type gives out light radially, whilst the 'flat' type tends to give out most of its light above and below. Choose an appropriately shaped bulb according to what type of lamp it is.

Keeping Warm
Having lived in houses with no heating and no hot water, I know how unpleasant an experience it can

be. For many, especially those on a low income, heating is a serious drain on the finances. It is essential for the elderly and young children to be warm, if not they may be vulnerable to illnesses that could be potentially life threatening. If you are on a low income you may be eligible for financial assistance from the government to help with your heating bills. The Energy Efficiency Office's Home Energy Efficiency Scheme (HEES) provides grants to people who are over the age of 60 or on a low income. At present £198.70 is the maximum allowed for loft insulation and £128.50 for draught proofing. There are grants and schemes that are available, but some people are unaware of the help to which they are entitled, or they are too proud to ask for it.

If you are about to have your electricity or gas cut off because you are having trouble finding the money, try to contact them before they do anything. They can be fairly understanding providing that you inform them of your situation. If they know you are having difficulty paying they may give you an extended period to pay them off. If you do nothing it is likely they will just cut you off.

Many companies insist that prepayment meters are fitted if you have had trouble in the past in paying your bill. At least with a meter it is impossible to spend more than you use. One word of warning: if you are going away make sure that the meter has enough credits to last the time you are away. I know people who have lost the contents of their freezer because the electricity ran out while they were absent.

It is all very well turning on the heat, but if you are not careful all that warmth will disappear quite literally into thin air. Before the start of the next winter think over how you could cut down your heating bills; what measures you could take; how much they would cost; and whether they would be cost effective. Many of these money and energy saving ideas can be instigated with a minimum of fuss and expense, many just require a little thought!

Top tips on preventing heat loss:

● Place tin foil behind radiators so that the heat is reflected away from the wall and into the room. A lot of heat is lost as it transfers directly from the radiator to the outside wall. It is possible to purchase special foil from DIY stores but ordinary kitchen foil will do. It could save at least £5 to £10 per year on your heating bill.

● Loft insulation is essential. If your loft is already insulated but was done several years ago you might find that you can now buy even better insulating material. The insulating material should be at least 150mm thick, and can be fitted quite easily by a person handy at DIY. It should cost around £160 for the materials. If it is fitted by a professional it should cost around £120 plus the cost of the materials. The investment could be recouped in a couple of years by the amount of fuel saved if you fit it yourself, a little longer if you pay for someone else to do it. Don't forget that you will carry on making savings year after year.

● Stop draughts. Some houses, especially the older ones, suffer terribly from draughts, and yet draughts are one of the cheapest problems to rectify and savings of around £40 a year can be easily made. As much as 40% of heat is lost from a house through windows, floors and other gaps. Stop draughts coming through doors by fitting draft excluders, and around the bottom of doors place extra thick draught excluders. If your house is particularly draughty fit door curtains over front and back doors and even the letterbox. It is also important to fill in gaps between skirting boards and floorboards: a variety of materials can be used depending on the size of the gap, e.g. newspaper, beading or wood filler. Older style windows often let in draughts around the frames, so line them with plenty of draught excluder.

● Double glazing can help substantially to keep the heat within, and require less maintenance than wooden framed windows. It also cuts down external noise which is beneficial if you live close to a busy road.

● No doubt you are constantly being bombarded with calls from pushy double glazing salesman with tempting brochures, but think very carefully before you commit yourself. Fitting double glazing to a average sized family house costs over £5000. If you are only fitting double glazing because you want to save money you should bear in mind that it would take a whole lifetime to recover the installation costs from the savings on your fuel bill.

● If your windows need replacing anyway then it makes financial sense to opt for double glazing. It is possible to recoup the additional costs incurred, if not the entire cost.

● If you can't afford to fit double glazing then a cheaper alternative is secondary glazing. This costs around £300-400, can be made from plastic or glass, is easier to fit, and would save about £35-40 a year.

● If it is still too expensive to upgrade all the windows in this way, just fit secondary glazing in a couple of rooms, the ones you use the most. Alternatively, produce your own secondary glazing using cling film. Special wide film can be bought from hardware stores so that a window can be covered with one piece. Attach the cling film to the window frame with double sided tape, then heat with a hair dryer to stretch it tight and remove wrinkles. The result may not look stylish, but it provides an extra barrier between the cold outside air and the warm air indoors.

● Pull curtains across as soon as it is dusk. Remember: don't just close the curtains in the rooms you are in, close them too in all the rooms you are not using in order to minimise draughts and the cooling effect of cold window panes on warm air. However, when the sun is shining don't forget that it provides an excellent source of heat, even on very cold days, and if you have a particularly sunny room make sure you leave the doors leading to it open so that the heat can filter through to the rest of the house.

• The floors is another area that is susceptible to heat loss. Use rugs or preferably carpets as much as possible and the thicker the underlay the better.

• Lag the hot water tank with its own jacket. If it already has one but it is thin then replace it or even better put the new one on top of the old one. The jacket should be at least 80mm thick and conform to the British Standard 5615.

• Eat plenty of warming food. Winter is the ideal time for wholesome stews, porridge etc.

• Wear extra layers of clothes. It is better to wear several thin layers than one thick one.

• Fit extra thick curtain linings, or purchase special thermal lining.

• If you have a loft make sure that you keep the trap door to the loft closed. If it is left open in the winter the warm air from your heating will rise straight up and through the roof. Don't forget to insulate the back of the trap door.

• Board up old fire places that are not in use.

• Make efficient use of your central heating. The most effective method of control is to use a programmer, which allows accurate control over hot water and heating. Most simple programmers can only control whether the system is on or off, but there may be times when you just want hot water or just heating so it is worth investing in a programmer that gives this type of control.

• A shelf above a radiator can help deflect the warm air to rise outwards instead of straight up where the heat will be quickly lost. It could save you between £5 and £10 a year.

> # Turning down your thermostat by 1 degree for the whole year could save up to 10% on your heating bill

Auctions

Going, going, gone. Yet another bargain goes under the hammer. When the word 'auction' is usually mentioned people tend to make associations with fine antiques or cars and believe they are normally only frequented by people 'in the trade'. If you are of this belief think again: auctions are for everyone.

There is normally at least one auction house in each major town or city. Auction houses are used as a quick and convenient means of selling goods. Some auction houses specialise in a particular area of goods, eg cars, antiques, or even wine. The most common type has a mixture of goods, usually a selection of household effects ranging from washing machines, sofas, tables, to more diverse items such as stuffed animals, old cricket bats and top hats. The nice thing about an auction is the diversity of the items for sale. It is definitely the place to find unusual things.

As a rule, auction houses are regularly used by trades people. They are where many antique dealers and car dealers get their stock. The presence of dealers at auctions actually keeps the prices low because they have to put a margin on any goods they buy and sell to the general public so they can make a profit. Auction prices only get high when collectors are present. They are unconcerned with resale values and want an item at any price. Most

people, though, stop bidding if the price gets close
to the normal market value. If you are smart then
you will go along to the auctions and get yourself a
bargain.

Auctions will normally be advertised in local papers
a few weeks before the sale and the goods can be

viewed prior to the sale. Catalogues of all the items in the sale are normally available for a small fee, and some auction houses only admit people if they have bought a catalogue.

The next stage is to read the catalogue. If there is anything of interest go and check the condition of the item. If you are wondering how much it is roughly worth ask for an estimate, as this will give a good idea of how much the auctioneers expect it to go for. This is only a guideline, on occasions when someone is very keen to have a certain object they might bid well over the estimated price. The golden rule of buying at an auction is always to set yourself a limit and don't go over it. It is very easy to get carried away and come away with things that perhaps you did not really want.

Occasionally you will find that there are certain lots for which no one will bid, so if you are the only person bidding you can often get a real bargain. Usually the best time for bargains is at the end of the auction when there tends to be fewer people to compete with, so prices are generally lower.

Remember that when you buy from an auction there is normally a commission fee of 10% and on certain items you will have to pay VAT.

When you make a bid for an item (called a lot), you are offering a stated sum for the lot. If anyone offers a higher sum, your offer is no longer valid.

But if the auctioneer accepts your offer by banging his hammer, you have entered a legally binding contract to purchase the lot, and you can't change your mind at the end of the sale.

Perhaps the most risky auctions are those dealing in cars. You have a very short period of time to decide if you want to buy a particular car and you don't get a test drive. If you have little knowledge of cars go with someone who has. You might end up driving home in what you think is a bargain, but is what they in the trade call a real lemon.

At some auctions they give information about the car. This can tell you:

● Where it has come from, i.e. was it a privately owned or a company car?

● If it has a service history.

● The condition of the engine, gearbox, steering, etc.

Such information is normally only given on more expensive cars. At the cheaper end of the market they usually have no history, no MOT and quite often they don't even start. It is amusing to watch an auctioneer trying to sell a car that is being pushed past his nose because it won't start. Another thing to look out for is whether you have any rights should the car turn out to be stolen or have an outstanding hire purchase agreement on it. Some people end up losing their car and their money when they find that the car they bought was in fact stolen. Even though you might have bought the car 'in good faith' you have no legal standing and the car must be returned. At some auction houses you pay a fixed fee of around £20 to cover you against any such problem.

Buying a house

The biggest one off purchase that most people make in their life is when they buy a house. If you are feeling really brave why not buy a house from an auction? At present, due to the number of repossessions that are still occurring, there is an increasing number of homes coming up at auction. If you are bidding for a house, it is imperative that you have seen the house, seen a surveyors report and are 100% sure that you want to live there. This is not the same as buying a second hand sofa: you have been warned!

Look out for auctions of goods from the Police, British Rail, and the Post Office as they all hold auctions of lost property that has remained unclaimed after a certain period.

Never get carried away at an auction by bidding for more than you really will be happy paying and don't forget that in addition you have to pay commission and VAT on some goods

---

Travel

Ever since passing my driving test at the age of 18, the once cherished bicycle that provided years of virtually free transport was destined for the garage and has hardly moved in years. (It also kept me fit . . . that alas has also gone by the wayside). 'So what?' you might be asking. Well, if you are determined to save money, an appraisal of your travel methods must be undertaken.

Here are some tips:

● Keep your car regularly serviced: it will be more economical.

● Enrolling in a evening class in car maintenance could save you hundreds of pounds every year if you do your own servicing.

● Replace worn out parts with parts from a car scrap yard or buy reconditioned parts. The only rule is never use second-hand parts where it might jeopardise the safety of you and your car.

● If you travel by train to work make sure that you purchase a travel card.

● Travel by train is cheaper at certain times. Try to organise your journey so that you travel during the cheapest period.

● Coach travel is normally cheaper than rail.

• If you are travelling by car, plan your route to prevent losing your way, incurring unnecessary fuel costs.

• Listen to travel information to avoid heavy congestion areas.

Car Sharing

As the country's roads get increasingly congested and pollution causes irreversible damage to the environment we must begin to look at more ways of reducing traffic. One option is car sharing, which involves giving neighbours lifts to work. The petrol costs can be shared, saving you and your fellow passengers money, and it lowers the number of cars on the road.

Car sharing does not have to be solely for work. It can work efficiently for taking children to school or to clubs, shopping trips etc.

Buying a new car

I still find it unbelievable that so many people buy new cars. I can see the appeal of going along to a car showroom and picking out the car you want with the all the options that you think are necessary, having the pleasure of it being truly your car, and enjoying that new car smell that permeates from the interior. But have you considered how much a new car is actually going to cost you? You will obviously be aware of the purchase price of the car, but what about factors such as depreciation and ease of resale?

It is not uncommon for people on a modest income to borrow over £10,000 for a new car. Not only is borrowing costly, but that first year of owning a new car is incredibly expensive due to depreciation. Nearly all cars are liable to depreciation; only a few cars, normally classics, are able to escape this costly condition (many classics actually appreciate in value).

The depreciation rate for cars varies from make to make and even from model to model. Certain models such as Mercedes are renowned for their high resale value, but there are others whose value drops at alarming rates. The average price of a family saloon car is currently around £11,000 and in the first year you would lose around 35% of its value and in the second year 17%. The level then slows down to around 12% per year after that.

So in that first year you would lose roughly £3850, which works out at £320 a month. If you are trying to save money never buy a new car. The price you pay for being its first owner and choosing the colour you want is the equivalent to a luxury holiday or another car.

If you still insist on buying a new car here are a few tips that could save you money:

• Always negotiate on the price. As a rule you should be able to get at least 10% knocked off. Putting a little effort into haggling could save you thousands, but many people are embarrassed to negotiate a price and therefore pay heavily for a quiet life. Once you get the hang of it you will find it enjoyable and one of the best ways to save money.

Don't spend too much on optional extras. These days cars come pretty well equipped, and any extra you pay for will be worth a fraction of its true value when it comes to selling the car.

> **Before buying a new car think about how much it will depreciate in its first year and what else you could do with that money**

• Avoid choosing a peculiar colour. If ease of resale is an important aspect of buying a new car, remember that some colours are easier to sell than others. Red cars are the most popular, and as a result will be worth fractionally more than similar models in other colours when it comes to selling them. Exotic colour schemes may appeal to you, but it could be hard finding someone with similar colour tastes when you want to sell.

● Before you buy a new car find out how well it holds its value. You can check this by purchasing a guide to second hand car prices. Check to see how much the value of the car you are after fell on the basis of last year's model. The figures normally work on the car covering the average mileage for a year, which is around 12,000. If you drive fewer miles then your car will not depreciate so quickly, and vice versa. Certain cars hold their value well and others seem to lose their value at an alarming rate. So when buying a car don't just think about its performance and breathtaking lines, think about how much it is really going to cost you.

Buying a second-hand car

The second hand car scene often receives unfavourable press. Stories frequently appear in the papers about unfortunate people who have bought a car second hand and then later found that it is actually two halves of separate cars welded together. Although caution must be used in buying a second hand car not all of the dealers are like the television character Arthur Daley. Ask around for recommendations, as there are always well respected businesses and individual dealers in the trade.

As with new cars, the price quoted by the salesman would normally be well in excess of his minimum profit margin. He will try this ridiculous price in the hope that you might be sufficiently gullible to pay it: don't make his day . . . haggle. If you are unsure of the average price for that particular model, use one of the various guides that are available from newsagents giving a comprehensive list of new and used car prices for nearly all makes and models.

Insurance Group
As insurance premiums seem to be increasing every year, make sure that you know what insurance group the car you intend to buy is classified under. The higher the group the more it is going to cost. A car's insurance rating is determined by the size of the engine, performance, cost of repairs etc.

One important point is that if you purchase a car that has been modified in any way it is vital to declare it to your insurers. Even if you are unaware of a modification you might find that you are not covered in the event of a claim if the insurance company discovers a relevant modification upon investigating the claim. There have been cases of people being refused payouts from their insurers even for failing to tell them that they had added 'go faster stripes'. The reason is that modifications such as alloy wheels or spoilers make cars look 'better' than the basic model, and therefore more desirable to thieves or joyriders. This means that they are at a higher risk of being stolen than a basic model, and an insurance company needs to know these facts before deciding what level of premium to charge. If the company is not informed of all the facts at the time the insurance is arranged, the contract is invalid. A claim arising from an accident rather than theft from a vehicle which is subsequently discovered to be a higher theft risk due to a modification but not to have been a higher accident risk will be invalid. Even though the modification was not a cause of the accident it will nevertheless invalidate the insurance.

Shop around for insurance quotes because prices can vary by hundreds of pounds. Don't just blindly renew your policy each year. Just before your policy is to be renewed get some other quotes, so that when you are sent your renewal quote you can compare it. Your own insurance company may then try to match it, rather than lose your custom.

An alternative to buying from a dealer is to buy from a private vendor. Cars are always advertised in the local paper or on noticeboards. As with buying any car there are certain things to look out for. One of the rules of buying a secondhand car is always to stick to your principles, don't be swayed into buying something that you are not utterly convinced you want.

What to look for when buying a second hand car:

The Exterior

● Look for any obvious signs that the car has been involved in an accident.

● Check the alignment of the panels, see that the doors and bonnet fit flush.

● See if there are signs of major repair work, welding, or replacement panels. A replacement panel will often be a slightly different shade in colour as the old paint work will have faded.

● Look for indications of minor repairs in the bodywork i.e. where it has been filled and then resprayed. Unless the job is well done these areas have a habit of recurring. I once had a Morris Minor that was more filler than metal and required extensive patching at least once a year!

● Check the condition of the exhaust system, and the wear on the tyres.

● Check that the tyres have worn evenly. If one is worn more than another the tracking is probably out.

● Check that there are no leaks of fluid from brakes, shock absorbers, petrol tank, and under the engine etc.

● Check for rust in important areas such as by the suspension mounts. If there is a lot of rust it may require welding to pass its next MOT.

> Not all car salesmen wearing thick sheepskin coats are unscrupulous, just don't be persuaded into buying anything that you don't really want. If you go out looking for a small runabout don't come home with a Chieftain tank!

● Check the sills for indications of rust as these are vital to the structural integrity of the vehicle.

The Engine

The engine is an expensive component, and if it needs replacing on an old car it could cost more than the car is worth. So what should you look for? This advice is only designed to give you a few approximate guidelines: if you really don't have any knowledge of cars take someone with you who does.

● Before starting the engine, open the bonnet and check the condition of the oil. It is better if it is translucent rather than black or sludgy.

● Ensure that there is sufficient water in the radiator, and check that it is not rust-coloured.

● After starting the engine listen for any rattles or shakes. It should tick over well, and not splutter or judder when revved.

● Look out for excessive or bluish smoke from the exhaust. This is always a bad sign and usually indicates that the piston rings are worn (they will not pass the MOT in that condition and are expensive to replace).

Steering
● Check for excessive play in the steering. If there is a delay between turning the steering wheel and the wheel moving there could be a problem with the steering column.

Gearbox
● Check that all the gears operate smoothly and do not jump out of gear when accelerating or decelerating sharply.

Brakes
● Check for wear of the brake shoes if they are visible. If you take the car for a test drive test the brakes and make sure that they do not pull the car excessively to one side.

Interior
● Check for rips in the cloth, and cigarette burns in the seats. A common problem is a worn driver's seat.

Clocking
This is an expression that refers to the illegal practice of winding back the odometer to make the car appear as if it has done fewer miles than it really has. This is unfortunately a relatively common problem. To help check that the mileage is correct, look at the service history: the mileage should have been recorded on service records and the MOT certificate.

• Look for heavy wear on the pedals and carpet on the driver's side. Genuine low mileage cars do not normally have threadbare carpets where the driver's heel has rubbed it, but if you are unsure it would be better to find another car.

• Always try to buy a car that has at least 6 months MOT.

• Don't buy a car with very high mileage unless it is very good value.

• Be wary if there is no service history. It is better to pay a little extra for a car that has a comprehensive service history than to buy a cheaper car with only a few or no details.

Saving On Car Bills

Petrol or diesel?
The vast majority of cars in Britain are petrol based. However in Belgium diesel cars are as easy to find as somnolent octogenarians in the House of Lords. Europe is full of diesel cars, so why are we in Britain the odd ones out? The cost of diesel fuel might be a factor. In most of Europe diesel is far cheaper than petrol. In the UK whilst being cheaper than Four Star it is usually priced as the same as unleaded petrol.

Diesel cars are noisier than petrol ones, but they are a great deal quieter than they used to be. Diesel emissions are smokier than petrol, but contain fewer harmful elements.

The bottom line is that they are generally cheaper to run. On average a diesel uses 25% less fuel than the equivalent petrol model, and diesel is still cheaper than most types of petrol.

Servicing and running costs can be lower for diesel vehicles, and the lack of spark plugs makes them more reliable for starting in cold or damp conditions. The only drawback is that they are more expensive to purchase either new or secondhand.

Running Your Car For Less

Indulgence in motoring is not without its costs, both financial and environmental. There are, however, many ways to reduce your motoring costs and decrease the detrimental effects your car has upon the environment. Here are a few tips:

● Buy your fuel from a supermarket, where the prices are normally lower than roadside filling stations. Remember to fill up before you go on a motorway: their prices are extortionate.

● Treat your car and your passengers delicately. Accelerate gently and don't pretend that you are about to start a Grand Prix race at each set of traffic lights. Gentle acceleration, braking and cornering will reduce fuel consumption and extend the life of tyres, brakes and engine components.

● Make sure that you use the appropriate gear. Keeping the revs low by using the highest appropriate gear reduces fuel consumption. Never cruise in fourth gear if you have five gears.

● Remember to push the choke back in as soon as the engine has warmed up. Running the vehicle with the choke out when the engine is at full running temperature not only uses excess fuel but can cause engine problems.

● Don't carry heavy items in the car unless you need them. The heavier the car the more fuel will be needed to overcome its inertia when accelerating.

● If you are stuck in a traffic jam or at a railway crossing for longer than a couple of minutes, turn off your engine.

● Keeping your car well maintained will make it more efficient, producing fewer harmful emissions.

● If your car does not run on unleaded petrol (cars built after 1991 can use unleaded fuel without adjustment), think about having it converted. It is worthwhile to make the change because unleaded is significantly cheaper than leaded petrol and if you drive many miles, are going to keep the car for some time or care about the environment, you will save money as well as reducing harmful emissions.

• Drive at a lower speed especially on motorways. You use 30% more fuel driving at 70mph than you would do if you drove at 50mph.

• Keep the tyres at the correct pressure: if your tyres are under-inflated by 7psi or more you could be wasting half a gallon of fuel per tank.

• If you have a roofrack that can be removed, take it off when it is not needed as it makes the car less aerodynamic and hence will use more fuel.

• An incorrectly adjusted carburettor can cause a huge increase in fuel consumption. Another reason for keeping your car well serviced is that it is less likely to break down and leave you stranded. Although you can never predict when you are likely to break down, if you do and are not a member of a rescue service then it could cost you a great deal of time and money.

• It is cheaper to buy 12 months tax instead of buying two 6 months discs.

• If you are not using your car for a few months you can reclaim some money by sending your tax back to the DVLC with the appropriate form from the post office.

• When your car is in need of repair try a number of garages before deciding which one to use. Main dealer garages often charge more than double that of small local garages.

• Be sure to instruct the garage to call you before performing any work that you have not instructed them to do. It is easier to negotiate before they start than after they have finished.

• If you think that the garage has not fixed what they had agreed to do, take your car back and make sure that they put it right.

• If, when given a bill, you think it is excessive, ask them why it is so high. It is always a good idea to ask them for an estimate before they start the work, even for small jobs.

Car servicing costs consist of parts and labour. The labour charge is normally fixed, whilst the parts can vary in price depending on whether they are 'genuine' (being the same make as was originally fitted), or are parts made by independent companies.

So what is the difference? Perhaps the first point is the difference in price. If you get your car serviced at a franchised dealership, then you would normally end up paying a higher labour charge and more for parts as they would always fit genuine parts where possible. There is nothing wrong with this except that if non genuine parts were fitted at an independent garage you would expect to save anything from 10% to 500% depending on the part being replaced. Some items such as replacement wings can offer savings of hundreds of pounds if the non genuine parts are used. Don't think that by using non genuine parts you will be jeopardising your safety: all parts have to be approved and are normally identical to the 'real thing'. If a garage makes comments such as only genuine parts should be used, ask them why, and get an independent second opinion.

A new car will normally come with a manufacturer's warranty. If something goes wrong during the period of the warranty you can return the car to the garage to have them rectify the problem. Legally they are not obliged to repair the car, but in practice they will. Many people feel obliged to take their car to the dealership to have their car serviced whilst it is under warranty, but this is not necessary. However, if a fault arises due to work carried out by another garage you cannot then take the car back to the dealership and expect them to fix it.

Extended Warranties
As with most products it is now possible to take out extended warranties, which come into effect when the original warranty expires. They are different from the original warranties in that they are legally binding. But before taking out an extended warranty on a car, think carefully. They can be very expensive and the main drawback is that they normally stipulate that you are tied to having your car serviced at the garage with whom you have the warranty. If it is a main dealer it could cost you hundreds of pounds extra in servicing over the period of the warranty.

Communication

Telephones

If you have teenage children you probably wish that Alexander Bell had not been so clever and invented such a such a costly instrument. For many years British Telecom had a monopoly on the supply of the telephone service, but today there are some alternatives. The standard telephone bill arrives quarterly and is usually accompanied by gasps of horror as to its ever increasing amount. Help is at hand, as there is money to be saved in reviewing your choice of service.

The first thing to consider is the phone itself. Are you still renting a phone from British Telecom? If the answer is 'yes', then send it back to them. Modern telephones can be bought for as little as £8 so after less than one year you would have saved money by not renting a phone from BT. If you still have the old type of sockets there is a charge of around £30 to fit the new one.

Cutting down the phone bill

Depending on the size of your average quarterly phone bill there is a number of options that could save you money. BT offers services designed specifically for heavy and light users. Option 15 is for heavy users, who have large phone bills. At present for a £4.99 quarterly charge you receive a discount of 10% off all direct calls. There are also special schemes for business users.

Although having an itemised bill can invade privacy it is a good way of monitoring usage. If you have children, especially teenagers with friends abroad, you will know exactly how much they have been costing you. If you are feeling particularly Scrooge-like you can deduct the amount from their pocket money!

• Having an itemised bill is normally the most efficient way of reducing the length of phone calls, as you are more aware when you are making the call that it will show up on the bill.

• Have a stopwatch by the phone so you can see for how long you have been on the phone.

• It is possible to prevent your phone from being used to dial premium rate numbers which can cost up to 50 pence a minute. Contact BT for further advice.

• Remember that when you phone a mobile phone it is much more expensive than phoning a land line.

• Try to make phonecalls during off peak periods.

The majority of the nation still uses BT, but companies such as Mercury and Cable companies are taking a greater share of the market. If 'cable' is available in your area they can supply a phone line at the same time, and you will have no further need for BT. Some of the cable companies offer free off peak calls to other cable users in the area. This is ideal for a person who makes many calls locally and at off peak times.

Mercury was formed in the 1980s and has struggled to make an impression against one of the most powerful companies in the country. They use BT lines as it would be uneconomical to have two sets of lines, and they also have phonebooths which are cheaper than BT's. Mercury is a service that is used in conjunction with BT's. For a small quarterly charge, you can save 20% on all long distance calls routed via Mercury.

Mobile phones

As these phones become cheaper and more accessible to everyone, it is important to be aware of the different tariffs and services available. Those who expect to make a large number of peak rate calls can opt for a tariff that combines a high monthly rental charge with low cost peak rate calls. If you expect to use it mostly for incoming calls, a lower monthly charge is available with higher priced calls. Some tariffs charge per second used, while others round up to the nearest thirty seconds or minute, the latter being more expensive. Some services have limited geographic coverage, and their prices tend to be correspondingly low.

Whichever tariff you are on, using a mobile phone is much more expensive than a land line phone, so use with care.

As well as choosing the most economical tariff, there is currently a choice of digital or analogue services. Digital services offer clearer sound quality and some degree of 'future proofing' at a higher cost. Analogue services are cheaper but will be obsolete in a few years, and will eventually require replacement.

Finance

It is hard to get through life without having to use a financial institution such as a bank or building society, although some people do manage it. The differences between banks and building societies are reducing each year with a number of building societies now having bank status and offering the same services. For simplicity the word 'bank' will be used to cover both type of institutions.

Banks offer a wide range of services, including a safe place to keep your money, cheque books, direct debit, standing order facilities, money lending, financial advice, stockbroking, pensions and life insurance. The banks are very keen to expand their non-banking services such as insurance and are quite aggressive with their marketing tactics.

The major high street banks are always telling us that we should be banking with them instead of with the opposition. They are all characterised by one line slogans, such as 'The Listening Bank', or 'The Bank That Likes To Say Yes'. But in reality they are all much the same, and when you have money they are only too willing to say 'yes' but it is usually a completely different story when the money runs out.

Before selecting in which bank to deposit your hard earned money it is worth taking a little time to choose. The 'Big Four' (Barclays, Natwest, Lloyds and Midland) have branches in practically every town in the country, and though each branch of one particular bank should offer the same service as any other, it does not appear to work like that. Much depends on the staff working at a particular bank, and if you are able to build up a good rapport with your banker, you will find it easier to borrow money.

Personal contact is vital for a good relationship with your bank. If they know you only as a set of figures on their computer, there will be no room for leniency should you suddenly go overdrawn without authorisation or find yourself with any other financial problems. If they know nothing of your character and reliability they will act strictly according to the rulebook when it comes to charging the highest possible penalties. If you are known to them as someone who is not going to default on money owed, you will be treated with more trust and respect, and will not have to pay such high penalties. Becoming personally known to and developing a good relationship with your bank manager will normally save you money in the long run.

> # Developing a good rapport with your bank can only work in your favour

Saving your money

There are still people who simply do not trust banks and building societies and would rather keep their money hidden in the house or garden. Is this a sign of eccentricity and foolishness or are they merely wise in not trusting the banks or building societies? The overnight collapse of Barings, Britain's oldest merchant bank, demonstrated that even a solid looking worldwide banking organisation can topple like a house of cards, taking with it the funds of all the 'little people' who trusted it.

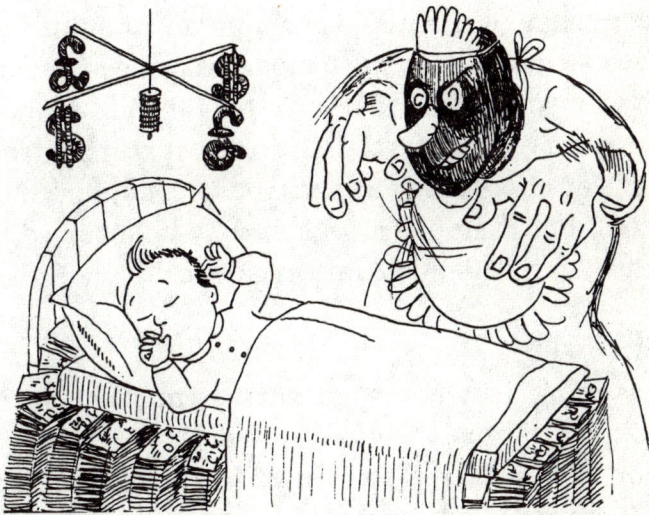

Once you have deposited your money in the bank, you normally assume that it is safe, nonetheless. This it may be true, but whether you would approve of the way your bank spends your money is another matter. Some banks make a point of avoiding investing their funds in countries run by oppressive regimes with poor human rights records, but many banks judge investments purely on financial criteria.

There are many different types of bank accounts, but basically they can be divided into current accounts and savings accounts.

Current accounts are for everyday usage, your money is instantly accessible but you will receive little or no interest on the money in your account.

Deposit or saving accounts are available with a huge range of facilities depending on a number of factors, such as how much money is being invested, how long it is going to be invested for and whether you want easy access to the money. It is important that you choose the most suitable account for your needs. For example, a penalty may be incurred if money is withdrawn at short notice.

Borrowing

It is much easier now to borrow money which makes it all too easy to rely on the banks if you are short of money. If credit is used sensibly it can help with budgeting, but many people find that if they are offered the opportunity to borrow money they do so, but find repaying it more difficult.

Before borrowing any money decide how much you really need to borrow and, perhaps more importantly, whether you can afford the repayments. Borrowing money is expensive: if any organisation lends you money they will want to earn a profit from the deal.

Banks

The normal choices through the banks are in the forms of overdrafts or loans.

Overdrafts

Overdrafts tend to be for short term borrowing, (up to a year), or for regular short dips into the red. Certain bank accounts offer a small free overdraft which is useful if you are always slightly short at the end of the month. Make sure that your overdraft is authorised, otherwise you be will be heavily penalised for going overdrawn.

Loans

A loan is normally for a minimum of one year, but repayments can be spread over many years. Normally the larger the sum borrowed the longer you can have to pay it off. Interest rates tend to be lower for the larger amounts.

Other sources

Private finance companies advertise heavily, offering money to all. However they are often very expensive and such an agreement should not be entered into without first trying other sources. Before you enter into a loan agreement find out exactly how much you are paying, not only per month but what percentage interest per annum this works out at. It is common to see companies advertising to lend money, quoting figures in terms of monthly payments, with the annual percentage rate in small type. This is misleading: the amount they are quoting for repayment sounds more affordable than it really is.

Always find out what the annual percentage rate is, don't just look at how much the monthly repayments are

---

Store finance
Many of the high street stores now offer their own credit facilities and store cards. They even give instant credit, so if you have several of these cards your debts can soon begin to get out of hand. It is also worth remembering that in general it is cheaper to use a standard credit card as opposed to a store card. One plus point of store cards is that they sometimes have special offers for cardholders, such as shopping evenings for cardholders only or discounts, but generally if you are trying to save money avoid cards of this nature.

The other alternative to a store card is to use their credit instalment facilities. You can pay off the purchase with monthly payments: this again is an expensive way of borrowing, so try your bank first.

Do you check your statements?
I still find it hard to open my bank statements each month. They can sit there for a couple of days before I summon the courage to take a look; when I finally do open them I tend to glance with squinted eyes in the hope that the news will not cause too much pain. However, after a few days of coming to terms with the balance, it is important to check the statement for any errors. It is incredible how many errors are made. Studies have found that as many as one in eight customers are charged incorrectly each year by their bank.

To help prove any anomalies it is important to keep receipts of purchases so that you can check the amounts you have spent against those on your statement. If you discover any discrepancies contact your bank immediately.

If the bank credited you with more money than it should have done, you might think that it is your lucky day. Unfortunately they usually spot their own mistakes and help themselves to the money directly from the account. If you have already spent it or are heading for Mexico, they will do their very best to get their money back, to which they are entitled. If they credit you erroneously and you spend or keep the money whilst being aware of the mistake, you are guilty of theft, so it pays to be honest in these situations.

If you have arranged an overdraft or some other type of borrowing facility make sure that you get the details in writing, e.g. how much interest you are paying, when it has to be paid off, etc. This way if there is any disagreement you have something more solid than a verbal agreement.

Finally, if the bank has made an error with your account and you have to spend time and money rectifying this mistake, try to get some form of compensation from the bank. They are only too happy to charge for letters they write to you, so why not do the same to them? Invoice them for the same amount they would charge you if the error had been your own.

Investments

If you have surplus money as a result of all the economies in this book and you can refrain from spending it, why not invest? Once you have made the decision to do so, and have decided how much money you are going to put into the investment, you have to decide where you are going to invest, for what period of time and how much risk you are willing to take.

RACE HORSE SHARES

It is this risk element that will determine where you invest your money. If you are looking for a safe investment it is unlikely that it will produce a high return. Normally the higher the risk the higher the potential return. It is sensible to spread your investment in a number of areas, some low risk, some medium and some high. Just remember that if you invest in a high risk venture you could end up with nothing. Investing in a high risk venture is akin to gambling and should be viewed with the same rule - never invest more than you can afford to lose.

● Low risk - Banks, building societies, National Savings, premium bonds

● Medium risk - Unit trusts, Personal Equity Plans (PEPS), Investment bonds

● High risk - Shares, Business Expansion Scheme

Although investing in shares is risky there are often other fringe benefits. For instance, if you own a certain number of shares in P&O you can get cheap ferry crossings.

One recommended method of saving is through the Tax-Excempt Special Savings Accounts (TESSAs). This allows you to invest to invest up to £9,000 over a 5 year period. At the end of five years you would receive the interest tax free, the rate of which will vary from bank to bank.

Before investing always seek
professional financial advice,
and be wary of people you
meet in the pub who tell you
of a great opportunity to
invest in a new venture

Insurance

The purpose of insurance is to protect ourselves financially against the possible occurrence of undesirable and/or costly events. In other words, it limits life's gambles. It is possible to insure almost anything. Professional musicians, for example, might insure their hands so if they were involved in an accident in which their hands were damaged the extent that they could no longer play to a high standard, they would receive a payout from the insurance company.

The insurance companies have to work out the risk involved, i.e. the likelihood of that event occurring. If the risk is a large one, the premium paid will be high, and if they believe there is a low chance of that event occurring then this will be reflected in a lower premium.

House and Building Insurance

In case you do not have your contents or house insured because you feel that you just cannot afford it, you are taking a huge risk. Although the aim of this book is to save you as much money as possible, it certainly does not advocate taking these sorts of risks in order to save money. Many people who are not insured are short of money and decide to take a chance. When they are then burgled they find themselves in a dire situation. It would be advisable to sacrifice other pleasures instead of forsaking basics such as insurance.

It is up to you to keep up with insurance payments. It is a familiar story to hear of people who go to claim on their insurance only to be told that their policy is void due to a failure to keep up the payments. This can be devastating to families as the insurance companies do not tend to respond to 'sob stories'.

That's the warning over! It's time to return to the issue of saving some money. Very few people when they are sent their renewal notices for insurance do anything but return it with the payment. This is exactly what they are hoping you will do. As with many of the ideas for saving money in this book, a little effort is all that is required to make economies: for the sake of half on hour or so you could save yourself hundreds of pounds.

The process is simple. After receiving your quote, phone a few reputable insurance firms and ask for a comparable quote. I would almost be prepared to guarantee that anyone could make some saving if they tried this. If, or should I say when, you get a cheaper quote, phone up your existing insurer and tell them that you are going to take your business elsewhere as you have found a more competitive price for the same cover. They will be reluctant to lose your custom and should try to beat the quote you have been given. If they cannot match it, take out a new policy and congratulate yourself on saving money. Don't forget to do the same thing next year, as it can vary from year to year as to who offers the best deals.

Types of policy
There are a couple of basic house contents policies:

● The first is calculated by the value of your contents, referred to as sum insured policies.

● The second type is calculated by the number of bedrooms a property has. In this instance you do not have to calculate the value of the house contents. With this type of policy you are insured for a fixed amount, say £40,000 for a 4 bedroom house. However, if the value of your contents is only £30,000 you are over insuring yourself and you can be sure that this will cost you money. It is more sensible to work out the value of your contents so that you know exactly what you are paying for.

Not all the policies give the same cover so check the policy you have covers all of your requirements. Certain items such as valuable musical instruments would normally have to be insured separately.

Life insurance
The future remains a mystery, life events cannot be planned or controlled. Efforts can be made to shape our lives, for example having a healthy

lifestyle should mean that you live longer, but there are no guarantees. If you have people who are financially dependent on you, life insurance is the most obvious choice for giving you and your dependants financial peace of mind in the event of redundancy, illness or death. As with all insurance policies there are different types that can be taken out according to your needs. It is essential when you are trying to save money that you do not sacrifice things such as life insurance.

Personal pensions

We all look forward to the time when we can retire from work and spend our time exactly how we please. To be able to enjoy your retirement you need money, and this requires financial planning. At the age of retirement everyone is currently entitled to a basic state pension, but it falls way below what would be needed to live a life of luxury. If you have paid full rate National Insurance contributions as an employee you may be entitled to an additional pension from the State Earnings Related Pension Scheme (SERPS). As well as this you can have a pension which is organised through your place of work or you can have your own personal pension.

In 1988 there was a change to the system, giving people the chance to opt out of SERPS. The state still makes a contribution, but will contribute to a scheme chosen by yourself. This means that you have more freedom, but also that you have to decide which scheme you believe to be appropriate for your future requirements.

Choosing a pension scheme is no different to choosing any other purchase: there is a vast range and some are better value than others. It is impossible to give advice as to which would be the most suitable pension for everyone as there are too many variables. One piece of advice is always to seek the help of an independent financial adviser and think carefully about what your requirements are, how much you want to pay into the scheme, what you expect out of it, etc.

There are two basic types of adviser, 'independent' and 'tied'. An independent agent offers policies from a number of companies, whereas a 'tied' agent is, as the name implies, tied to the policies of one particular company.

The golden rule is never rush into any financial commitment, and compare prices as there are always good deals and bad deals. Take the time to find a 'good deal' as you could be paying into a scheme for most of your working life. Remember that there is a 14 day 'cooling-off' period after signing for a personal pension scheme, which gives you the opportunity to cancel the agreement. There is an exception to this - if you are transferring rights from a former employer's scheme to a personal pension, there is no 'cooling-off' period.

Security

You might wonder why there is a section on security in a book about saving money. Well, there is a connection. There is no point in making an effort to save money if you are going risk the contents of your house through poor security. We all hope that it will never happen to us, but there is no sense in taking a risk when there is so much at stake.

It is alarming how many burglaries occur every year. The British Crime Survey puts the figure at close to one and three quarter million. They are a reality for everyone. It is tragic that after working hard to buy your possessions someone can just come along and help themselves. Not only is the loss of property distressing, the intrusion into your home is for many a psychological burden that can stay for years.

The risk of burglary is higher where the population is denser, such as in the inner cities, but clearly not everyone can move to a rural area simply to reduce this risk. The best way to avoid being burgled is to take appropriate security precautions. Although they will not guarantee your protection they can lessen the chance of a break-in.

The majority of burglaries are committed by the opportunist thief, who will look for certain indicators in a house and then decide if it is worth taking a risk, e.g. are there any windows left open, or is the house surrounded by tall fences or hedges giving plenty of cover? A burglar will look for the house that appears to be an easy target and has little chance of him being discovered.

Here are a few crime facts:
- About 50% of burglaries occur during the day

- About 80% occur when there is no one at home.

- The rear of the house is the most popular point of access for burglars, either through the back door or windows.

There are certain items that burglars tend to go for, and most of the time they are limited to what they can carry. Although there have been stories where thieves have left houses bare, including taking the radiators, sinks and toilets, fortunately thieves are not normally this organised. The following are among the most popular items stolen:

- Televisions
- Videos
- Cash / credit cards
- Jewellery
- Stereos
- Camcorders
- Cameras
- Computers
- Compact discs

As the statistics show, the chances of being burgled are now too high merely to be regarded as an unlikely eventuality, so it is vital to take security precautions. As Lord Baden Powell said to his scouts, 'Be prepared'. The more precautions you take the less risk you have of being burgled.

Here are a few security tips:
- Fit window locks to all easily accessible windows.

- A five lever mortice lock, plus a cylinder lock should be fixed to the front door.

- A lever mortice sashlock should be fitted to the back door, and a good heavy duty bolt.

• Put locks and secure bolts on all French windows.

• Keep tools and ladders secure so that they cannot be used by burglars to help them gain access.

• Fit timer switches to lights so that it appears you are in at all times. The more you have the greater the illusion.

An unsecured house is like an invitation to a burglar. Secure your house now!

• Do not leave valuable items in view.

• Remember to cancel milk whilst away.

• Inform neighbours if you are going away so that they can keep an eye on your property.

• Join a neighbourhood watch scheme.

• Photograph valuables, so that if you are burgled you have proof of what you owned.

It is a good idea to keep the receipts of all valuable goods as it helps with the insurance claim. Make sure the receipts are in a safe place; if they get stolen, it will make it harder to claim on your insurance and it will also benefit the burglar.

Be extra vigilant at Christmas as this is a favourite time for burglars. There is nothing more distressing than having all your presents stolen, especially if you have young children who will be distraught if they lose their toys.

Alarms

If you are thinking about installing an alarm system, make sure that you get a reputable company to install it. There are many different services available, and many companies charge an annual fee. Some of the more expensive alarms send a message to the police if the alarm is activated. Having an alarm is not a guarantee that you will not get burgled, but it might reduce the chances. Insurance companies usually offer a discount on homes that are secured to a certain standard. Apart from protecting your home, thorough security could protect you and your family, as well as providing peace of mind.

Con-men

Apart from the common 'break and entering' types of burglary, some thieves are more canny. There has been an increase in the number of bogus callers, particularly those who pose as bogus officials, such as representatives of the council or electricity board, or even as policemen. They often wear the appropriate uniforms and have fake identification, making it hard to distinguish between impostors and the 'real thing'. This type of criminal usually preys on the elderly who are less likely to notice the difference. If you ever suspect an official caller to be an impostor under no circumstances let them into your house. Call the official organisation they are claiming to be from and check they have sent someone out or that the ID they have belongs to one of their employees. It is sensible to have a door chain fitted so you can check their identity before letting them in. If you go off to phone for verification of their integrity keep the door closed, as a genuine caller will not mind you taking this precaution.

It is not just bogus officials you have to watch out for. There are people who go from door to door offering to buy 'antiques' or other items. They are normally con merchants who will pay you a fraction of the true value of the item. Don't be fooled by their stories, sometimes they can be very persuasive. If you are interested in selling any items such as antiques or jewellery have them valued by a reputable dealer first. You might own an item such as a small vase that you think is worthless but turns out to be worth hundreds or even thousands of pounds. It would be a shame to let a 'dodgy dealer' give you a few pounds for it when he knows perfectly well its true value.

Also be aware of 'cowboy' workmen who travel around the country persuading people to have unnecessary work carried out on their homes. The standard of work tends to be poor, and they will be almost impossible to track down subsequently.

Entertainment and Leisure

Life is to be enjoyed. For some a perfect day's relaxation might involve a twelve mile walk, while for others it might be to sit in front of the television. There are literally thousands of ways of spending your time in order to relax: some may require money, others might be free. If you are short on money then it is a good idea to try to limit the number of activities you do that cost money and try to indulge in those pursuits that are free.

• Instead of going out to the cinema, which can cost easily £15 for a family of four depending where you are, hire a video. To make it more like the cinema turn the lights down low, make your own pop corn and hot-dogs, and arrange for someone to sit behind you and talk throughout the film.

• Don't forget to make use of the countryside while it's still free. When was the last time you went for a walk? Children love going on walks and it is a great way to introduce to them to nature, as well as being good for the health.

• Look out for free concerts which are usually advertised in local papers. They can take place in churches, village halls or in open public places. Just because the entertainment is free doesn't make it inferior to concerts you have to pay for, so make the most of them.

Eating out is hard to beat. It gives you the opportunity to let someone else worry about the cooking, the serving and the washing up. You are made to feel special, and the meal will be free from the interruptions of home. In this country, though, eating out is an expensive luxury. This is a shame because on the continent eating out is much cheaper and is therefore enjoyed more frequently.

So how can you save money if you still want to eat out? Look out for restaurants that offer special deals, like two for the price of one. Pizza restaurants and fast food chains are particularly good in this respect.

• Remember it is usually cheaper to order a set menu rather than ordering à la carte. If you are trying to economise it would certainly not spoil the occasion if instead of ordering three courses you just have two or share the third. You might find that you enjoy the meal more because you will not leave the restaurant feeling bloated.

• Another way of saving money on entertainment is to consider buying stand-by tickets for shows. Most theatres and concerts will have a number of reduced price tickets that are available on the day of the performance, and they can be as little as half price. This is a great way of seeing live events on the cheap. For some popular shows, however, there will be a big demand for seats, and you take the risk of not getting any tickets.

> # Look out for cheap tickets for shows and concerts, but check that the seats are not situated behind a pillar

• If you are meant to be getting tickets for a special occasion then it is not worth taking any risk. There may be no guarantee of success, and you might end up having to buy them from a ticket tout who will charge you much more than the face value of the ticket. This is, of course, something that you should not be doing if you are trying to save money. Planning ahead to get tickets for a popular show will avoid you having later to pay the rising 'market' price touted tickets.

Holidays

It is usual to start planning a holiday having just returned from one. The thought of a holiday is what keeps many people going in their jobs. It does not always matter if the holiday is a week in the Bahamas or a couple of days in Clacton, it is just nice to get away.

A week on holiday is normally going to cost more than a week of ordinary living, even if you are staying with friends. There are ways to make savings, giving you the chance either to have more spending money or the opportunity to save for your next holiday. Here are some ideas to cut down the expense of taking a holiday. Bon voyage!

Late Availability
Those who are afraid of taking a gamble are often the first to complain that they never get any bargains. Unfortunately, you normally have to be prepared to take some sort of risk in order to get a 'good deal' whatever it might be, and this is half the fun.

If you can be fairly flexible as to when and where you go, prepare to save a lot of money. Most tour operators heavily discount holidays that they have not sold close to the time of departure. Some deals occur a few weeks prior to the start of the holiday whilst others can give just 24 hours notice. The longer you leave it the more money you are likely to save, and the less choice you are likely to have. Some of the most frequent destinations that are reduced in price are holidays to Spain, Portugal and Tenerife, but quite frequently holidays to Tunisia, Gambia and the U.S.A. turn up as bargains. In fact, a tour agent with a holiday almost anywhere could be desperate to sell the final seats on the plane or rooms in the hotel at a knockdown price in order to diminish possible losses.

The place to look out for cut price holidays is of course in your local travel agency. They are often in the window, but if you don't see any it is worth asking. One of the best places to find a cheap package holiday is on the teletext pages of the television. There are normally numerous companies offering rock bottom deals. If you are thinking of booking a holiday over the phone for a late availability holiday there are some points to check first.

It is a good idea to have a few brochures with you so you can compare the original price of the holiday against what they are offering. You can also use the brochure to see if there is a picture of the accommodation, as it will probably be your only chance of seeing it, otherwise you are taking a gamble.

On the subject of taking a gamble, many of these special cheap deals suffer from a few drawbacks. Quite often, although you might know where you are going, it could be the case that the accommodation will be decided when you arrive. You would normally be informed of the minimum grade, e.g. the lowest you would be put in would be a 3 star but you might be lucky and be put in a 4 star. The problem with this is that hotels vary greatly and you might end up miles from where you really want to be. On the other hand you might be paying for a 3 star and end up in a luxurious 4 star. Before you book this type of holiday think carefully about how much of a risk you are prepared to take. Many people take this type of holiday as a second or even third holiday and they are happy to be anywhere that is away from home.

It is not only holidays that are discounted. It is also possible to obtain late availability flights at a reduced price. Again check with your travel agent, teletext or travel pages of the newspapers.

If package tours are not your scene and you fancy a cheap holiday, have you considered a house swap? There are companies that arrange exchanges, i.e. you let people use your house whilst you are away and you use theirs. Theoretically you could be staying in Florida, whilst an American family has the pleasure of experiencing a summer holiday in your home. It might sound a little strange, and conjure up visions of coming home and finding your house destroyed, but the companies that organise these exchanges usually try to vet the clients and deposits must be left in case of damage. The exchange company charges a fee for arranging the swap. Bear in mind that a swap would normally be between similar types of properties.

If you have friends abroad why not suggest a swap with them? It means that all you have to pay for are the travel expenses and food.

If you have a large family or like to holiday with friends another option is to rent a large house. In France, for instance, a beautiful Chateau that could sleep 15 people complete with a swimming pool would be cheaper to rent per person than four families renting smaller individual holiday homes.

A large group of friends on holiday can be great fun, with barbecues and pool parties. If there are a number of families the children can keep each other amused leaving you the chance to relax for a change. Parents can take it in turns to organise things for the children and even the cooking can be done in rotation. One word of warning: make sure that you really get on with these friends, because the day in day out intimacy can cause friction

Another possibility is staying at home. Going on holiday does not always turn out to be the relaxing stress free period that it is supposed to be. A holiday can often be most traumatic due to missed flights, delays, noisy hotels, bad food, sickness, theft, dissatisfied children, etc. Sounds familiar? So why not leave all that upheaval behind, stay at home, and use all the money you have saved for buying luxuries in which you would not normally indulge. Treat yourself: go to the local Italian Restaurant and have a bottle of Chianti each night. By the end of the 'holiday' you might even think you are in Italy!

One other reason for staying at home is to take the time to discover some of Britain. OK, the weather is variable at the best of times, but the scenery is as beautiful as any in Europe.

The Wedding

It is referred to as the 'happiest day of your life', and it will also be one of the most expensive! Many people spend vast sums of money in order to make it that perfect day, but is it all necessary? The actual wedding day goes so fast that is often hard to appreciate all the effort that went into planning it.

A wedding does not have to cost a fortune to be memorable

It is the ambition of most brides to have the 'dream wedding', with everything planned to the last detail. Weddings in Britain appear to differ to those in many European countries, who take a more casual attitude to the 'Big Day'. This book is not trying to tell you how to plan your wedding, as it is a personal affair, but bear in mind that after the wedding money is usually tight. There are ways of keeping the costs of a wedding down without making too many sacrifices. You could save money in certain areas and spend it on something else connected with the wedding. You may feel, however, that you would rather spend as much as you can afford (or more), which is understandable.

The following are the main costs of a wedding:

- Clothes
- Hiring the church
- Invitations
- Photographer
- The reception location
- Food and drink
- Flowers
- Transport
- Honeymoon

Clothes

A wedding is the perfect opportunity to dress up, not only for the bride and groom but for the guests too. Brides can spend months looking for the dress that will bring tears to the eyes of the guests and hopefully to the groom as well. Wedding dresses can cost thousands of pounds, or just a few hundred: however much it costs, for a dress that would normally only be worn once it is a lot of money.

There is the option to rent and although you would not have the pleasure of showing your children your wedding dress and wishing you could still get into it, it would save you money. One advantage of renting is that you could hire a most exquisite dress for a lot less than buying an inexpensive dress.

Other options include buying a dress so you have the delight of knowing that you are the first person ever to wear it, then selling it after the wedding to recoup some of the money. Alternatively why not buy a used dress from an agency specialising in secondhand wedding dresses?

The groom, if going for the traditional morning suit, would nearly always hire an outfit, but many people who are on a tight budget are using the money they would have spent on hiring a suit to buy a new suit that they can wear after the wedding.

The Venue
The church normally makes a charge for its use and if you want a choir it will cost even more. Even if the wedding is in a registry office there will be a charge. There is not much scope for saving money here.

The Invitations
Making a wedding list involves spending hours wondering who to invite and who not to invite, and this always causes friction. When the list is completed the invitations need to be printed. It will save you money if you can typeset and print them on a home computer with desktop publishing software, or if you know someone who can do it for you. Gold embossed invitations are not vital: save cash by choosing a nice typeface but printing with black ink on white paper.

Transport
Rather than turning up to the church in an ordinary car, most people hire something a little special. The

choice is normally something like a large luxury car or a classic such as an old Bentley. If you want to save some money why not try to find a friend with a classic car who would be willing to drive you for free? Another alternative is to approach a classic car club in your area and ask if any members with a classic car could offer you a reasonable deal.

The Reception
Depending on the budget there will be certain parameters as to what type of reception you hold. At the budget end of the scale is a DIY reception held at home, a close second would be a village hall or function room at a pub.

Hotels are the most expensive option but are ideal for receptions as they can often organise the whole event, including food, drinks, toastmaster, and disco if required and it is convenient for putting up guests who are staying. Most hotels offer special packages depending on the services required. If you wish to cut the bill you could have a cold buffet, but if you are feeling extravagant you could go for a three or four course meal. Bear in mind that there is normally room for negotiation whatever you choose.

Don't forget that if you are planning on having a reception for 50 guests, the hotel will not want to lose the chance of getting your custom. If they won't budge on the price of the food try to get them to throw in some free drinks. If they refuse to make any concessions try to get some other quotes from similar hotels, as they will vary dramatically in price. Choosing where to have the reception is a big decision and it is important that you are going to be happy with your choice. Unfortunately a hefty price tag will not always guarantee high quality, so think carefully before you commit yourself and your guests.

If you have a large garden, the wedding is in the summer, and you have a great deal of faith in British weather, then why not have an al fresco reception? I went to a beautiful wedding in France where the reception was held in a garden overlooking the Pyrenees. The food was kept simple: salads and cheeses etc, but this was washed down with an inexhaustible supply of local wine. The guests were seated at long trestle tables which were borrowed from a local school, and people served themselves. It was one of the most memorable weddings I have ever been to: the secret was the weather and the breathtaking views and the refreshing lack of formality.

If you decide to hold your own reception why not take a trip to France and stock up on wine and beer? A barbecue can be a fun, straightforward and cheap way of feeding wedding guests at summer receptions.

Keeping The Children Amused

We have all been told stories of the bygone days when children were given a hoop and a stick to play with, and if they were lucky they had a bag of marbles or a lump of coal. This was a far cry from the current world of computer games and the latest space toys.

One of the main contemporary problems is that many toys are merchandise products derived from films or television programmes. Whatever might be in vogue one month could well be out the next when a new super hero arrives. A popular cartoon or television series might be accompanied by a range of products such as toys, books, stickers, clothes or even food.

Children display a remarkable degree of persistence when it comes to trying to make parents purchase these products. It is all very well if you can afford to indulge your children with all that they want, but for those with a low budget or even a moderate wage it is just not possible as these items are far from cheap. Trying to teach your children the value of money and instil in them a sense of control is all part of being a parent. Children have to learn that they cannot have everything they desire because life unfortunately is not quite like that, although explaining this to a young child is never easy.

Keeping a child amused does not have to cost a great deal of money. We may laugh at recollections of how children were kept amused in the past, but perhaps we have just forgotten how much fun could be had without incurring great expense? Many of the old pastimes and games have been lost in a haze of television and computers. Just remember that personal computers have only been around for about ten years! People might argue that keeping children amused has always been expensive, but at least computer technology tends to fall in price as it improves in quality, and there are many fine multimedia educational packages available now which will become less expensive as time goes on.

For those who are not enthusiasts of the computer age, here are a few reminders of how to keep the little darlings amused for next to nothing (or even nothing at all):

Face paints
These are usually available from joke shops or toy shops. Children can spend hours painting their faces, though they find it even more amusing if you let them paint yours!

Dressing up box
No family should be without a dressing up box. Simple outfits can be made such as cowboy's, Indian's, nurse's, and soldier's. Children enjoy putting on adult clothes, especially hats and wigs.

Papier mâché

All that is required for this is flour, water and paper. By covering objects in layers of paper with the 'glue' all sorts of things can be made, which can then be painted.

Poster Paints

How about trying to encourage your child to paint? All children have a penchant for painting pictures. All you need is set of poster paints that are mixed with water (very sensible when they cover you and themselves in paint), brushes and some large sheets of paper. Children also enjoy painting with their hands, or another alternative is to make shapes from potatoes that can then be dipped in paint and used to print shapes.

Traditional Party Games

Sardines

This game is normally played by children but adults have been known to play it. It needs at least five players and a house. All the players congregate in one room. One player is sent off to hide, the lights are turned off if it is dark, and then the other players leave and try to find the first 'sardine' (The hidden player). The idea of the game is for another player to find the first sardine and they join them in their hiding place. If you discover the sardine when there are other players around you should pretend that you have not seen them, but return later and hide when the coast is clear. The game is over when all the players are hiding in the same place, if that is possible!

Musical Statues

All you need for this party game is some music. The guests all dance when the music is playing, but when the music stops they must pose in the position they are in at that moment. The controller of the music then goes round looking at the statues, checking for signs of movement. Whoever moves first is eliminated, and then the music starts again and the remaining players continue dancing. This carries on until there is only one player left and they are then the winner. Once the players are eliminated they can try to make the remaining players move by trying to make them laugh.

Mummies

This is a classic game that will certainly bring about much amusement whether it is played by children or adults. It requires several teams of two, and a roll of white toilet paper for each team. A time limit is set, usually about two minutes, during which one member of each team has to cover the other head to toe in paper, trying to recreate the look of an Egyptian Mummy. The winner is the most authentic looking mummy.

Chopsticks

All you need for this game is a bag of frozen peas and several pairs of chopsticks. Each player is given a pair of chopsticks and a plate of frozen peas. The idea is for the players to try to transfer the peas from the plate they are on to another dish within one minute. The winner is the person who has managed to transfer the most peas. (This game is not suitable for young children as they are unlikely to be able to use chopsticks).

Musical Bumps

A slight variation to musical chairs. The guests are required to dance around whilst music is being played, then when the music stops the children must quickly sit down on the floor with their legs crossed. The last one to do this is eliminated. This carries on until only one person is left.

Hunt the Thimble

One player is chosen to hide an object whilst the other players are out of the room. It does not have to be a thimble - it can be any small object, but it is important that the object is still on view and accessible. The other players then return to the room to hunt the thimble. When a player spots the hidden object they must sit down. The last player to spot the object is the loser.

Cold, Warm, Hot

One player is nominated to leave the room, while the others hide an object. Once the object is hidden the player who left the room returns. He must then try and find the hidden object. The other players given him clues by saying 'Warm' if he is near the object or 'Cold' if he moves away from the object. As he gets nearer the object the temperature rises, eg. warm, hot, very hot, until the object is located.

Apple Bobbing

This is traditional at Halloween, but it can be played at any time of year. A large bowl, usually a washing up bowl, is filled with water. Depending on how cruel you are feeling you can make the water cold or warm! A number of apples are then put in the water. Players have to kneel in front of the bowl, with their hands behind their backs, and try to extract an apple using only their teeth. This is not as easy as it might seem, unless you are brave and dunk your head right in. The first player to retrieve an apple is the winner. Be warned: this game can get out of hand, and it is advisable to place towels around the edge of the bowl to absorb the inevitable spillage. Make sure an adult is around if young children are playing.

Bun on a string

This is a similar game to apple bobbing: it involves suspending a number of buns from the ceiling with pieces of string. The buns must hang down at a height that is accessible to the children. The children must then try to eat the buns without using their fingers. This can be very amusing to watch, but keep an eye out for cheats!

The final game is a personal favourite, and although normally played by children, I have recollections of playing this at student parties whilst at University. I am unsure of the correct title to this game, but here are the rules:

A number of dressing up items are required, such as hats, gloves and scarf, a die, a very large bar of chocolate on a plate and a knife and fork. The players must sit on the floor in a circle and roll the die in turn. If a player throws a six they must put on the items of clothing and try to eat the chocolate piece by piece with the knife and fork, until another player throws a six, when he must put the clothing on and do the same. The game continues until all the chocolate has been eaten.

Entitlements

Social Security

The social security system is designed to offer assistance to people under certain circumstances. It covers a number of areas such as child benefit, income support, unemployment benefit, and housing benefit. The list is almost as large as the number of forms that you normally have to complete for each benefit. Some of these forms are complicated to fill in, but unless you fill them in you won't get any money.

Each year there are millions of pounds of benefits that are unclaimed, and there are also millions of pounds of benefits that are claimed illegally. The difference is that in the latter case the government does their best to track down the culprits, but it makes no such effort to try to help those people who are entitled to benefits but do not realise it.

Some benefits are available to families regardless of status and income, such as child benefit, while others are means tested. Means tested benefits are given according to your financial position: they are not always related to income because it depends also on how many dependants you have and if you have any savings.

There are far too many benefits to list in this book, and in any case there is frequent legislation adding, deleting or modifying them, so it is always advisable to contact your local security office or Citizens' Advice Bureau if you are in doubt as to whether you are eligible for any help. Unemployment benefit is only given to those who have paid sufficient National Insurance contributions. If you have not paid enough National Insurance you will only be entitled to Income Support.

Unemployed

Being out of work brings with it many hardships, not only a lack of money, but also a loss of dignity and pride. Saving money is usually very important to those on benefit as money is usually in short supply. Make sure that you are claiming all the benefits you are entitled to.

It is possible to get help with the cost of going to an interview if you satisfy certain conditions. The help is meant for interviews that are away from home, i.e. beyond a normal daily travelling distance. You might also be eligible for the cost of up to two overnight stays. Make sure that you apply before you go away for an interview, as it is too late once you have already been.

Legal Aid

Certain professions are well paid because the skills offered are relatively scarce yet valuable to consumers. The knowledge possessed by legal practitioners is particularly expensive to access, yet vital for some aspects of life. Before you consult a solicitor get a few recommendations from friends, and find out how much they charge, as their rates do vary.

There is some good news, and the news is Legal Aid. Legal Aid is funded by the government and offers free or low cost legal help under certain circumstances. There is normally a number of solicitors in any town or city who carry out Legal Aid work. The deciding factor as to whether you are eligible for Legal Aid is normally related to income. It does not matter if you own a home or even have some savings, you might still receive some financial help.

It is the solicitor who works out if you qualify for Legal Aid. There is a system called the Green Form Scheme which is used for simple situations where advice is needed. If, however, you need representation in court, you would normally have to apply for Civil Legal Aid or Criminal Legal Aid. One point should be noted: if you manage to procure money or property as a result of winning the case, you might be asked to make a contribution to your solicitor's bill, and it goes back into the

Legal Aid Fund. This is called the statutory charge, and in these instances the Legal Aid is more like a loan, though of course it is paid back by court 'winnings' rather than out of your ordinary earnings.

Qualification for Legal Aid

There are certain limits on income and savings. If you are above these figures you would not normally qualify for Legal Aid. If you have a partner your income and savings will be counted as one, but there is an exception to this rule, which is when the case is between the two partners.

The amount of income and savings that is allowed depends on which type of Legal Aid you need to apply for. At the time of writing, if your disposable income is below £70 and you have savings of less than £1000 then you will qualify for help with the Green Form Scheme. For Civil or Criminal Legal Aid the allowances for both income and savings are higher, taking into consideration expenses such as rent or mortgage. At present the levels are a disposable income of £7,060 a year or less and savings of less than £6,750. There are exceptions to these rules, for instance pensioners are allowed to have more savings than this. The allowances change regularly, sometimes being raised to bring more people into the Legal Aid net, sometimes being shrunk to save money. It is always advisable to find out the most recent figures from a Citizens' Advice Bureau.

Here are a few other legal facts that might be useful:

● Everyone is entitled to free legal advice if they are being questioned at a police station, regardless of whether you have been arrested or not.

● Everyone is entitled to free legal advice on their first appearance at a Magistrate's Court.

● Many solicitors offer free or reduced cost first interviews under special schemes. Contact your local Citizens' Advice Bureau or the Solicitors' Regional Directory for more details.

Legal Aid Head Office
85 Gray's Inn Road
London
WC1X 8AA

Council Tax

No taxation policy has ever been popular: in the past there have been window taxes, clock taxes, and more recently the introduction of the 'Poll Tax' which came close to causing a revolt. We now have a replacement to the Poll Tax: the Council Tax, which is a little more popular. If you are wondering what the money you pay is used for, well, it is meant to help to pay for the local services that your council provides, though the levels of service and taxes vary from council to council.

The council tax works on a similar system to the old rating system, where the amount paid is related to the value of the property. The value of your property has been assessed by the Valuation Office Agency which is part of the Inland Revenue. There are eight council tax valuation bands.

Band Range of values at 1st April 1991
A   Up to £40,000
B   Over £40,000 and up to £52, 000
C   Over £52,000 and up to £68,000
D   Over £68,000 and up to £88,000
E   Over £88,000 and up to £120,000
F   Over £120,000 and up to £160,000
G   Over £160,000 and up to £320,000
H   Over £320,000

The banding of the houses was calculated from their value in 1991. Many people feel that they are in the wrong band, and are therefore paying too much (I don't think you would be complaining if your house was undervalued). Unfortunately it is too late to appeal against that decision if your house was banded under the 1991 valuation unless the government has plans to revalue all the homes in the country. There is a chance that you can appeal if you have just moved into the house, and there are six months within which time to appeal once you have moved in. It is also possible to appeal if there has been an alteration to the land near your home, for instance a new road. There are a number of free booklets that have been produced, in many different languages, on areas connected with the council tax that are available from social security offices or some post offices.

It is possible to get help with paying your council tax with council tax benefit. This is a social security benefit operated by local councils. Even if you are receiving no other social security benefit you still might be eligible for council tax benefit. There may be a discount on the council tax bill if there is only one adult in the house. If you feel you may be eligible for council tax benefit then contact your local social security office for advice.

The council tax must be paid by home owners and tenants. 'Homes' includes all types of dwellings such as houseboats and mobile homes. The appeals are dealt with by the local councils, but be warned it is a slow process. The first stage is to contact the 'listing office' where you can put forward your case. If the dispute is not resolved after 6 months then the case gets automatically referred to a valuation tribunal.

The most effective way of putting forward your case is to get a valuation of the property, which will cost between £20 and £100. Back this up with other evidence such as photographs of similar houses in the area that are in the lower band. There is one drawback, though: even if you win the case and your house is put in a lower band the council will not refund you the money you spent on the valuation.

Improvement Grants

There are not many instances where the government is willing to hand out money and they tend to stay pretty quiet about it, instead of informing those who might be eligible. Council tenants are now able to claim compensation for home improvements under the Citizen's Charter scheme. There are many different rules and regulations that apply depending upon what improvements are made. The compensation is paid when a tenancy agreement is ending or if a new landlord takes control of the property.

It is always advisable to get permission from the council before making any improvements so that no misunderstandings can occur.

The Right to Compensation was introduced in April 1994 and compensation is only given for work done after this date. There are quite a few stipulations, and interior decoration such as wallpapering is not covered, but there is a fairly generous list of useful or potentially money saving work that can be done, such as:

- Loft and cavity wall insulation
- Central heating or other types of heating
- Shower or bath
- Toilet or hand basin
- Double-glazing
- Rewiring
- Kitchen cupboards

- Insulation for water tank, pipes or cylinder
- Security devices, such as window locks, but not alarms
- Smoke detectors
- Thermostatic radiator valves

Claiming Compensation

There are some fairly strict rules that must be obeyed if you are considering claiming compensation. The compensation for work done is paid when you leave your home, you only have fourteen days in which to make a claim, so be prepared. In order for the council to make a payment they must have proof of where you were living, what improvements were made, how much they cost and when they were done.

How much money you will receive will depend on a number of factors. If some of the work was carried out with the aid of grants from the council you are not going to be able to claim anything as they were the ones who paid for it in the first place. If the grant did not cover the full amount, however, then you would be compensated for the money that you paid yourself.

The council also takes depreciation into account: the longer it is since the improvements were made the less compensation will be paid. The council also has the right to reduce the amount of compensation if they feel that the cost of the improvement was too high. The compensation includes the cost of the materials and labour, but not your own labour. There is a limit of £3000 for any one improvement, and no compensation will be given for work that cost less than £50.

To find out more information contact your local council's housing department.

Houses

Whatever type of house you live in it will always require some sort of repair. Usually the older the house, the more looking after it needs. So the problem is that as well as being expensive to buy, houses are also expensive to maintain. This section examines ways in which those costs can be reduced.

When house hunting the most important considerations are price, location, character, and size. Before buying a house it is important to sit down and consider all the possible implications.

Buying a house is usually the next step after renting, although some people are happy to rent all their lives as it they do not have to worry about mortgage increases or a fall in value of houses.

To buy a house you either need the money so that you can buy the house from the vendor, or you need someone who can lend you the required amount. A mortgage is the most usual method of borrowing money for a house. There are various types of mortgage and you need to speak to specialist mortgage consultants before deciding which is the best option. Remember that there are always deals available, and it is definitely worth spending some time negotiating.

When you are looking at a house think carefully about what condition it is in. Will you have to spend money on decorating, carpets and other fittings? What condition is the paintwork, window frames, eaves, gutters, or the roof? A surveyor's report is designed to point out any serious defects with the house, but they can miss things. Always check that the property you are interested in is not going to be in the vicinity of any new developments such as a new road or supermarket. If relevant information of this nature is withheld from you it is an offence.

> # Buying a house is a serious commitment, so make sure that you are ready for such a responsibility

When you have found your dream house the next stage is the bargaining. If you have never been one for haggling then this is the moment to start: you will not get many opportunities like this. The asking price for a house is usually set by the estate agents, and they will try to get as high a price as they think they can get away with. In no instance should you accept the first asking price, as it will normally be exaggerated. By offering a few thousand pounds less you are effectively putting that sum of money into your own pocket if the offer is accepted.

To aid you with your negotiation there are a few things that can help. Look at the price of similar houses in the area, and compare this to the one you are interested in. The next stage is to make a list of all the repairs that need to be done to the house. This is useful ammunition when asking for a reduction in the price. You can say, for instance, that the wiring is in need of repair and would require 'such and such amount' to put right. You could also say that you have found a similar house that has the extra benefit of an extension or a bigger garden but is the same price.

There is nearly always room for negotiation, but there is one word of warning: if the house is generating a great deal of interest you might lose it to another buyer, so be careful. One last piece of advice is that if the owners are leaving behind a number of fixtures and fittings make an offer on these separately from the bid for the house. You are in a strong bargaining position: remember that many of the items will be of little use to them, e.g. if they were to take the carpets it is unlikely they would fit the new home they have bought, so bargain hard! It would be difficult not to save money under these circumstances.

Making use of your house

Although the emphasis of this book is on saving money and time why not earn yourself a little extra cash? If you have a spare room in your house and would be willing to share it with a stranger why not consider taking in a lodger? There is always a demand for rooms, especially in towns and cities and it can be quite lucrative. The extra money that you receive will often cover all your bills, leaving you to spend your money on more pleasant sundries.

Before letting a room, decide what sort of arrangement you are going to offer: will the lodger have access to all areas of the house, or will they be confined to their room only? Will they have their own cooking facilities, share the kitchen or be provided with meals? It is worth getting professional advice before taking in a lodger, and it is useful to know your rights as well as those of a lodger. Finally, you might have to pay income tax on the earnings.

A similar alternative is to start offering bed and breakfast. This is slightly more complicated as there are certain rules and regulations that must be adhered to, regarding fire safety for example, but once these setup costs have been covered it can provide a useful source of extra income.

An Organised House

If you are already organised there will be no need for you to read this section, but, for those who are not, read on. Those who are not sure should think about the following questions.

• Do you know the location of your water stopcocks, gas stopcocks, central heating feed tank and system drain point etc?

• Do you have spare fuse wire, lightbulbs etc?

• Do you have access to a torch (that has working batteries in it)?

• Do you pay your bills on time?

• Do you have access to the telephone numbers of the gas, electricity and water emergency services?

• Do you have access to the telephone numbers of your doctor, local hospital, police station, solicitor, plumber etc?

• Do you have a first aid box?

• Do you have tools for the most basic jobs, especially tools that might be needed in an emergency?

• Do you keep your receipts and know where your guarantees are?

• Is your insurance still valid and do you have adequate cover?

If you answered no to more than three of those questions then perhaps you should consider reorganising your household. An organised house is an efficient, safe and more enjoyable place in which to live. If your house is organised, i.e. it is kept clean and tidy, it will save you time in the long run. It can be difficult to keep a house tidy, especially if you have young children (or any children, for that matter). One tip for keeping the house free of junk, is to have a box which you keep by the stairs where you can chuck things in that they leave lying around. Then threaten them that if any item stays in the box for more than three days it will be sent either to a charity shop or put in the bin. This never fails to make them tidy up!

An organised house is usually a safe house

Repairs to the home

Owning a house is a responsibility that must be taken seriously. During the last few years there has been a dramatic increase in do-it-yourself (DIY) stores, and this has obviously been accompanied by an increased interest in DIY. There are now numerous guides and manuals covering all aspects of DIY: projects for novices and projects for the more ambitious. Whether you are planning on changing a lightbulb or building your own extension they are a vital aid for any DIY enthusiast.

If you own your own house it is wise to keep it regularly maintained. It is far better to do regular maintenance rather than leaving it until there is a likelihood of serious damage being caused. For instance, if your window frames have started losing their paint and you ignore it year after year they will eventually rot as they have no protection, and will need replacing at great expense. But if you paint them when they first start flaking you will save yourself the expense of the new frames. There are hundreds of instances where people say 'Oh I'll fix it another day', and then they end up regretting it. A classic example of this, although not related to houses, is checking the oil in a car engine. I have known several people ruin their engines because they didn't carry out this simple check. This is learning the hard way!

Here are some examples of areas that need to be kept an eye on:

Roof
Check for loose or missing tiles. If a tile is missing and water gets in, it can cause extensive damage to the timbers, ceilings and wiring. So check regularly: this is one very important area that could end up costing you a fortune if you don't.

External woodwork
• Check the condition of windows, eaves, and weather boards. Paint regularly and treat or replace any rotting wood.

Walls
• Check for cracks, bulges, damp and make further investigations if deemed necessary.

Trees
• Prune large trees and make sure their roots are not doing any damage to the surrounding property.

Drainage
• Make sure all gutters and drains are kept clear.

Central heating
• Have your central heating system regularly serviced.

Chimney
• Have your chimney swept (please don't send your children up there, I believe it's no longer allowed!).

A house that is regularly and well maintained is less likely to develop any problems because hopefully they would be spotted before they get to be serious. This will definitely save you time and money in the long run. For those people who like to hope that it will never happen, think again, because if it does, there will be no one to blame but yourself.

Doing your own household maintenance is generally a good idea. It can be rewarding when you manage to complete a job to a satisfactory level, and it can of course save you money. DIY enthusiasts are often regarded as a slightly odd breed; this is perhaps a little unfair, though there are of course those who are obsessive about DIY and are not happy unless they are engaged in some type of project. There are limits to DIY and it is important that you don't try to be too ambitious: you could end up either causing more problems than you had originally, or compromising safety. Enthusiasts should never take risks, there are far too many accidents that occur through lack of care.

When contemplating a DIY project there are a number of points to consider:

• Do you have the knowledge and the capability to complete the project?

● Do you have the time to complete the project? It is no good starting on a project and then having to leave it half finished for months due to a lack of time.

● Do you have all the specialist tools that might be required for the job?

One other consideration is that if the project you are thinking of undertaking is time consuming, would be it be more sensible to get someone else to do the job if your time could be spent more efficiently doing something else? It is generally not worth taking time off work to carry out something like decorating if you could be earning more money by working and paying someone else to do it and still be better off.

There are certain jobs which are perfect for the even the most amateur DIY enthusiast, and by doing these you will save a great deal of money.

● Painting, internal and external

● Wallpapering

● Tiling

● Fitting cupboards

The average DIY enthusiast can do these things, but for more challenging projects the help of the professionals is required. This unfortunately means expense. Depending on the requirement, there are specialist trades, e.g. electricians for wiring jobs, carpenters for fitting doors, etc. There is also the general tradesman, the so called 'jack of all trades, master of none'! Choosing a tradesman is not easy, and there are a few important rules that must be adhered to:

Recommendations

This is often one of the best ways of choosing a tradesman. You can find out from friends certain information about people they might have used. It is a good idea to ask what they thought of the quality of the work done, did they stick to the price agreed, did they make a mess or cause any damage, were they helpful and honest? By getting recommendations you should generally avoid any firms that are not up to scratch, although there are never any guarantees that just because the people were recommended to you they are going to be reliable.

Yellow Pages

• There is normally a wide selection of trades people who advertise their services. However, you have no way of knowing the standard of service they provide.

Shop windows

• Many local shops have noticeboards which trades people use to advertise their services.

Trade organisations

● They will normally have a list of approved contractors who are qualified to carry out work relating to their profession.

Before contacting a tradesman work out exactly what your requirements are. Normally, the bigger the business, the larger the job they will undertake. Bear this in mind when choosing a contractor. A large building company is unlikely to want to come round and put up a couple of shelves, or if they do they will charge you an exorbitant fee.

Estimates

When you have found a number of suitable contractors, the next stage is to get them to give you an estimate for the proposed work. It is advisable to get at least three estimates from different contractors. To help with the estimate keep in mind the following guidelines:

● Write down what work you require.

● Specify which materials you want used.

● Make sure that you receive a written estimate, not a verbal one.

● Ask how long they will take to complete the work.

● Ask if there is a guarantee.

● Check when payment is required.

● Make sure there are no hidden extras such as equipment hire.

After you receive the various quotes, go through them comparing the prices and making sure that they are all quoting for the same materials and specifications. You will normally find that there will be one that is much more expensive than average, one that is much lower than average and several that are reasonable. It is not as simple as automatically choosing the one that gives the cheapest quote. If you know that the one who gave you the most expensive quote is a reputable and highly recommended builder it is difficult to know whether to pay the extra in the knowledge that you are paying for quality, but on the other hand there might be nothing wrong with the other builders and you might find that they are a lot cheaper. Try to find out some information about the different companies if you have not already done so.

Just remember that sometimes you do get what you pay for: anyone who remembers the chaos in the classic *Fawlty Towers* episode where Basil employs a cheap builder instead of the more expensive one his wife had told him to use will understand this point.

Who you choose is a personal decision, but bear in mind recommendations from other people. Many firms are successful due to their 'name' which is held in high regard and therefore they are unlikely to want to jeopardise this.

● Before you go ahead with your decision make sure you are totally clear about what is to be done.

● Read the estimate carefully checking all the small print. Make sure they are quoting for materials and labour, not just one or the other.

● Check that they have given you prices for the proper materials you require, not inferior ones.

● Make sure the contractor has adequate insurance.

● Find out if they are going to remove any debris which is left on completion, or will it be your responsibility.

● Does the estimate include VAT? A small firm might not be registered in which case it is not applicable and therefore cheaper.

The estimate is not a legally binding contract: for this you need a quote, which is much the same but it is legally binding. Never pay for the work in advance, a certain amount is fair for the purchase of materials, but if you pay all of it before they start work you will be in a very weak position if there are any problems.

Always get at least two estimates before choosing a contractor

---

When the work is completed there are certain things you must check, to make sure you are getting what you paid for:

● Check that they have completed all the work they were instructed to do, read through your estimate so you know exactly what they were supposed to have done.

● Check that the work is satisfactory, e.g. smooth plaster work, straight tiles, no leaks in new plumbing.

It is also important to check that they have used the materials that you have paid for. You might find that although you paid for a particular material it does not necessarily mean that it was used. This might mean that you are entitled to some money back and an explanation. You are entitled to be told of any changes that are to be made, as it is no good them informing you after they have already carried out the changes.

If you are not happy with the workmanship then say so. Far too many people are afraid to stand up for themselves. Write down what you are unhappy with and say that you expect it to be put right, or you will withhold the money you owe them.

Check for damage that may have occurred whilst building work was being carried out. It is inevitable that the odd scratch might appear here or there, but anything mildly serious should be noted and if it requires repairing, send the bill to the builders.

Running Your Own Business

There has been a dramatic rise in the number of people running their own businesses in the last decade, largely due to the changing employment situation. The eighties were a time of mass unemployment, and for many the only prospect of work was through working for themselves. Although many were successful the failure rate was very high and many people ended up back on the dole in a worse position.

The failure rate has now begun to slow down, but running your business is never an easy option. It normally requires total commitment which might mean working seven days a week and twelve hours a day at first. Most businesses require a certain amount of capital investment: how much you require depends on the nature of the business. The origin of this capital is normally either savings, redundancy money, bank loans or even a second mortgage, but whatever the source there is a lot to lose.

This book is designed to save you money and in line with that it must be stressed how important the planning stage is when considering starting your own business. Not wishing to sound pessimistic, running your own business is not always as glamourous as the image you may have conjured up. As was mentioned before, although the rate of insolvency has declined since the late eighties it is still a huge gamble and one of the easiest ways to lose money.

It is imperative that you investigate all the possible pitfalls that might occur, and always be prepared for the worst scenario, because it is likely to happen. Give some thought to what would happen if your business was to collapse: could you still provide for your family, would your home be at risk? Seek financial advice before you ever consider remortgaging your house to fund a business, in fact it is essential to seek guidance to help you with all your plans.

There are certain Enterprise Agencies that offer free advice to new businesses. They can offer a wide range of services and are normally run by retired businessmen who have years of valuable experience behind the advice they give. If you are running your own business and are unaware of the Enterprise Agencies then contact your local Citizens' Advice Bureau for more advice, as they could save you a fortune and make the difference between your business being a success or a failure.

> # Running your own business is a difficult option that requires complete dedication

If you are considering starting up your own business you may be eligible for financial assistance. If you are currently unemployed and have an idea for a business there are a couple of options. The government operates the Enterprise Allowance scheme which offers a basic wage for the first year, though not much. At present it is about £40 a week, but every contribution helps. Another source of help is from the Prince's Youth Business Trust, though there are certain stringent conditions which apply. You normally have to have been unemployed but there are exceptions. You have to be aged between 18 and 30 and have a reasonable business proposition. The Trust offers advice, grants of up to £1500 and loans on favourable terms of up to £5000.

Other alternatives include applying for grants from charities. There are literally thousands of charities that make grants to businesses every year. It is always worth trying find out if your business might be eligible, as you have nothing to lose except the price of a few stamps.

If you are already in business saving money is always a prime objective along with making money. It is amazing to look at the difference between the policies of different companies, however. Some companies are so lax in their spending controls that they go out of business. If your business is growing it is a good idea to start off with fairly strict controls.

Many employees abuse expense accounts and rarely make an effort to save money, usually because they feel there is no incentive for them to do so. If you are the boss then it is up to you to trim the fat.

Many companies lose thousands of pounds every year due to the misappropriation of simple items such as stationery or just blatant wastage. You might think 'what is the cost of a few pens and paper?' Well, if your company has only three employees the cost is probably not a great deal, but if your company was to grow to having a hundred employees then it would start adding up to a substantial amount. It can be hard trying to keep a track of all expenditure, and one idea is to make sure that your signature is required on any purchases you are worried about.

Your business might be able to help you save your money: if you do not use the services of an accountant because you think your business is too small, think again. It is probably worth paying one a visit. There are many ways to pay less tax, and an accountant can usually find a few loop holes to save you money. Utilisation of tax loopholes is not illegal, as opposed to tax evasion which is.

Index

Other books from Summersdale